THE NEW ORLEANS
VOODOO TAROT

The New Orleans Voodoo Tarot

Concept by
Louis Martinié and Sallie Ann Glassman

Text by
Louis Martinié

Artwork by
Sallie Ann Glassman

Destiny Books
Rochester, Vermont

Destiny Books
One Park Street
Rochester, Vermont 05767
www.destinybooks.com

Library of Congress Cataloging-in-Publication Data

Martinié, Louis, 1948–
      The New Orleans Voodoo tarot/Louis Martinié and Sallie Ann
   Glassman; artwork by Sallie Ann Glassman.
         p.   cm.
      Includes bibliographical references.
      ISBN 978-0-89281-363-6
      1. Tarot. 2. Voodooism—Louisiana—New Orleans—
Miscellanea.
      I. Glassman, Sallie Ann, 1954– . II. Title.
      BF 1879. T2M365 1992
      133.3'2424—dc20   92-4949
                                                                        CIP

Printed and bound in China

11 12 13 14 15

Text design by Virginia L. Scott and Bonnie Atwater

Destiny Books is a division of Inner Traditions International

To my husband, John Herasymiuk, whose heart drums a rhythm
for gods to walk across.

To Darius, who keeps us awake.

And to the loa, in hopes that they are well pleased.

Sallie Ann Glassman

To my companion, Mishlen.
You flow through this text
as does juice through a grape.

To the Lindenschmidts and Martiniés
with whose hands I write.

To all who helped and hindered this Working.
We are actors in a play so large
we know not its name.

Louis Martinié

ACKNOWLEDGMENTS

In Voodoo and many other esoteric traditions oral transmission is of great importance. The references to conversations throughout the text is an acknowledgment of this tradition of oral instruction. The spoken word feeds the printed word as streams feed a river. The references to conversations cited represent only a small share of what I was taught through the kindness of others. What I have been asked or sworn to keep secret has not found its way into this writing.

I thank Rose Frank, Joshua Frank, Muslima Moonpaki, Oswan Chamani, Miriam, Courtney Willis, Darius James, and Delphine, all of whom have shared important knowledge of the Voodoo with me. The loa speak through all of you. When I quote you, I quote them.

Thanks to Mishlen Linden, Joe Bounds, Marty Laubach, Owen Knight, Zain, Fred Fowler, Frater Turbator, Linda Falorio, Allala, Lairus, Bud Finger, and Nema, with whom I have worked the magicks for two decades. Your wisdom and your participation in the ongoing shaping of Western esoteric tradition is woven into the fabric of this book.

Thanks to Hymaneus Beta for planting the idea in the prolific artistic soul of Sallie Ann Glassman and also to the members of Kali Lodge, particularly Kenneth Wooten, Rebecca Frost, and John Herasymiuk, for assistance with the rituals.

A personal thanks to Leilah Wendel and Daniel Kemp for their help and encouragement.

Thanks to Cheryl Ito for her consideration and encouragement.

A special thanks to Cornelia Bland Wright, without whose careful editing this book would be incomprehensible even to me.

TO THE ANCESTORS

Joshua Frank was an old man when I first met him. He had served in the position of Obatalá in a ritual. His natural dignity and good humor made him a natural for Obatalá. I was fortunate enough to have a number of long conversations with him. He mixed family stories going back almost to slave times, anecdotes from his life, and a description of his understanding of spirit which developed over a long lifetime. It was a wild and rangy testimony to the power of the spirits. If I had read less and known more I would have listened better. The dry ink voices of published authorities took issue with his living words. It was hard for me to hear in the din.

His words and his presence stand as an example of the individual nature of New Orleans Voodoo. It is a family affair. His daughter Rose Frank is a practicing priestess who is trying to open a community center and a soup kitchen. New Orleans Voodoo goes back to the beginning and recaptures something very beautiful. In its wealth of shifting and sometimes conflicting detail and doctrine it matches the wide roamings of the human spirit.

To Joshua Frank, to all known ancestors, and to all those who came before and whose names are lost in the seas of time, I offer my efforts on this book.

CONTENTS

TWENTY-TWO ROADS & THE WILD CARD

FORTY SPIRITS

THE CARDS IN PRACTICE

INTRODUCTION

Also . . . the obeah and the wanga . . . these he shall learn and teach.
—Crowley, 1938

The procession of images which is the Tarot wound through Europe under the stewardship of the Gypsies, who carried with them the arcane knowledge of the great mystery schools of the Egyptians. This is what the teaching of Western esoteric tradition maintains. Portions of the knowledge of these mystery schools certainly find their origin in the elder interior regions of Africa, that area known to the Egyptians as "lands of the spirits."

From the green-canopied jungles, to the fertile plain awash with the Nile, to the towns and countryside of Europe, the pilgrimage of the Tarot stretched and plied its sacred route. The Voodoo Tarot which you now have partakes of the work of this procession. It stands as a strong reminder that Egypt is an African country whose advanced culture and religion rest upon a firm base of African theology. It is the mission of this Tarot to open a space for the "spirits" of the interior African lands, spoken of by the ancient Egyptians, to manifest and offer their seasoned advice.

These African spirits are the echoes of the human race's creation. They carry within themselves the how and the why of our existence. They are embedded in the deepest matrix of our consciousness, submerged leagues below the chatter of conscious thought. Spirits (a term popular in New Orleans), mysteries (les Mystères of Haitian use), and loa (a widely used Congo word and the term used here) are all used interchangeably to signify these vast forces.

The loa thrive in those places in-between, those places neither totally illuminated or totally of the dark. Outside of possession, the loa become most visible in the half-light of the Magic Mirror, that place where mind and matter join as one. The loas' ephemeral nature makes any effort to describe them seem obtuse; no definition can capture their shifting essence. "There are things not even discussed by oneself. . . . They must be left in the twilight and must not be looked at too exactly" (M. L. von Franz, 1972, p. 90).

In New Orleans the loa thrived under the general title of Voodoo. Voodoo is derived from a Dahomean word meaning spirits, and the Voodoo Tarot is an invocation of the Mysteries or Spirits which are the Voodoo. This Tarot is a tool we offer to these Great Mysteries. Through it They can begin to exercise their powers to teach, advise, and initiate into their deep and ancient wisdom. This Tarot is also a tribute to New Orleans, the Crescent City, at whose steamy breast the essence of Voodoo found nourishment and a link with the postindustrial present.

It is very important to keep in mind that this Tarot represents and mirrors a type and understanding of Voodoo developed in New Orleans. The outward practices, forms, and understandings that Voodoo takes are highly dependent upon place and the consciousness of the practitioners. There is no central organization to propose and impose an orthodoxy of expression. The spirits wear many masks and are expert at choosing the one that speaks directly to the heart and head of the voodooist. This book does not present *the* understanding of Voodoo; what it does do is give *one* understanding.

In New Orleans and elsewhere today, many Voodoo diviners use the Tarot to communicate with the loa. Our intention in developing the New Orleans Voodoo Tarot was to produce a deck that reflected Voodoo's multiracial nature and the special characteristics of the loa, thus making this form of divination a stronger one. The images and text that comprise this deck are largely influenced by a series of rites that we performed in New Orleans when contemplating this book. The purpose of these rites was to call and feed those loa and processes depicted here. The loa were asked to inspire within us the forms and words through which they wished to be represented in this Tarot.

The New Orleans Voodoo Tarot is a combination of traditional knowledge, personal insight, and the inspiration received through these rites. It is up to the user of the deck to assess the potency of this combination. This Tarot is meant to expand upon, not replace, the commonly held Golden Dawn-Thelemic interpretations of the cards. This gives the user a chance to transfer previous knowledge of the Tarot to situations where these cards are used and take advantage of Voodoo's delight in assimilating new esoteric accoutrements.

The deck was constructed as an act of service to the loa. May it form a link between those who use this Tarot and the great loa who have traveled so far and survived so much.

VOODOO: A PLAYING DEFINITION

Ernie K-Doh, a noted New Orleans R & B singer, once said, "I'm not sure, but I'm almost positive, that all music came from New Orleans." I also cannot say for sure that Voodoo began in New Orleans, but I can say that, more than any other city, New Orleans has influenced the development of Voodoo and fed its spirits. In Haiti it is common to speak of "serving the spirits"; the term "voodoo" is used to describe one type of rite and a particular dance, not the religious system as a whole. The use of "voodoo" to describe the whole of this religious system probably originated in New Orleans. Through the likes of Marie Laveau, the original Dr. John, and other famous voodooists, Voodoo grew to encompass more of the spirit, so that now New Orleans is associated more closely with the practice of Voodoo than any other city.

Voodoo is a syncretic merging of African, African-American, native American, and European beliefs and practices brought together by the early enslaved black population in order to feed the loa and survive. The loa are spirits, that is, sentient spiritual beings, who traveled the Middle Passage with the captured Africans and have taken firm root in the New World soil. Voodoo and the loa are always evolving; they manifest themselves in different ways in different cultural and geographic areas. There is no one right or wrong way to practice Voodoo, but there are ways that are more successful than others. This deck presents one successful way.

COMMON ELEMENTS OF VOODOO

Voodoo does not exclude, it includes.
—Darius James, 1989

There is an old story of two "experts" on neo-African religion attending a Voodoo ceremony and not at all realizing that what they are witnessing is a service for the loa, the spirits of Voodoo. This story points to a truth and a problem in speaking or writing about Voodoo.

The truth is that Voodoo is always evolving and has a voracious appetite when it comes to other religions. Much like its sacred snake, it swallows other systems of religious thought and practice whole. Voodoo's use of Roman Catholic imagery and ritual is well known, but this is only one example of the ability of Voodoo to enhance its liturgy through contact with other systems. One form of Voodoo takes on distinct east Asian religious characteristics, while another form posits Karl Marx as a candidate for loa. The saying "Voodoo does not exclude, it includes," embodies an important Voodoo characteristic so well that it is used as a leitmotiv throughout the book.

The problem is, How does one know what is or is not Voodoo? This is a particularly interesting question in a port city such as New Orleans, where many diverse cultural and religious elements come together without losing their unique identities. According to Rose, priestess of the Palo Myombe religion, members of seven different African tribes were brought as slaves to New Orleans. Each tribe brought its own traditions and rites of worship. The form of Voodoo now practiced in New Orleans is the result of the mingling of these traditions (conversation with Rose Frank, 1989).

Voodoo takes on a form specific to place and time. The Voodoo of New Orleans is not the Voodoo of Port au Prince in Haiti. The Voodoo practiced in New Orleans now is not the Voodoo practiced in New Orleans in the eighteenth century. The loa of Voodoo speak directly to the lives of its practitioners. The loa are in an intimate dance with their devotees. When conditions change, the loa change form (but not essence) in order to better meet the new physical and spiritual needs of their congregation.

With Voodoo there is no central force that defines orthodoxy, outside of the loa themselves. Each Voodoo temple or hounfor is a law unto itself, although there are certain elements that tend to mold or shape Voodoo in general. First and foremost, there is success: If a ritual technique works it will spread. Tradition also has its say: If a practice has been in use over a long period of time, then it has probably demonstrated its value. The ability to communicate the nature of the loa, to open up that connection between other people and the loa, can be a strong factor: Milo Rigaud, a writer and practitioner, is probably the most widely accepted authority. Lastly, there are widely known organizations such as the Technicians of the Sacred, the International Religious and Magical Order of Société, La Couleuvre Noire, and the Ordo Templi Orientis Antigua that, through journals and contacts, help to spread ideas and shape Voodoo practice.

Santería, like Voodoo, is an earth-related religion that makes much use of herbs and sacred stones. However, Santería is not Voodoo, and Voodoo is not Santería. The two religions each have a distinct thrust. The loa of Voodoo and the orisha of Santería are not interchangeable. An example of this are the guardians of entrances, Legba and Elegguá: Legba, of Voodoo, is the powerful elder, while Elegguá of Santería is an equally powerful childlike saint or spirit.

My experience with Voodoo points to a number of elements that define a service as Voodoo. A Voodoo ceremony will serve the Marassa, the Dead, and one or more of the loa. Legba will be called to open the door to the World of the Invisibles. These spirits and forces are described in the context of the Voodoo Tarot.

Sacrifice, be it animal, vegetable, mineral, liquid, or a subtle giving of the Priest or Priestess's energy, is part of every Voodoo ceremony. To sacrifice is literally to make sacred. The loa need food much in the same way as the living voodooist does. If, for instance, a cake is offered to Erzulie and the rite does not involve possession by her, she may only eat of the cake's essence, leaving the physical form for the voodooist or to be given to the poor.

Some form of possession will be present, either full or partial. The loa come into the world through members of their congregation. Possession ranges from the total possession common in Haiti to milder forms, where the loa direct or speak through a person.

The voodooist will always remind the congregation of the culture it is indebted to, either with a reference to Guinée, the Holy Land of the loa, or to the African roots of humanity, in particular black people. The type of beings that we are seem to have found origin in the African continent, and Voodoo songs and chants will often speak of returning there.

A voodooist generally possesses several qualities, the essence of which is embodied in the saying "The soul is only sure when it sings." The melody of the song is as old as the Mississippi, and the voodooist has a deep respect for the traditions that helped the melody to survive so long. The words flowing from the melody can be as new and creative as the Aquarium of the Americas located on the Mississippi's bank. This is not a contradiction; only growth and thoughtful change can ensure continuation and stability.

Connaissance is an important quality for the voodooist. It describes a deep knowing and a deep faith in the spirits. It is the surety of the soul, the positive knowledge that the loa will supply what is needed to those who honor them. It is the bridge between knowledge and intuition, an opening through which the loa speak, a grasp of the wild, untamed sense of things.

I was privileged to know an elder named Joshua Frank. His soul sang with a surety brilliant to behold; throughout his long life, with all its ups and downs, he demonstrated one quality that is foremost in the voodooist: he was a survivor. He took the worst that life and the dominant culture could give him and fashioned a creative and sustaining

Voodoo philosophy and world view. Honor to him who has seen so much: he now finds a place among the ancestors.

For me, these basic elements give some shape to what I call Voodoo. Each practitioner of Voodoo will use these elements differently and will develop a unique relationship to the loa. The important thing is not to let the parameters of Voodoo become so solid that they become unresponsive to the subtle molding of the loa.

THE ROLE OF SACRIFICE IN VOODOO

The act of sacrifice is integral to the practice of Voodoo. It creates a link between the loa and the voodooist, a link that reaches through the waters under the earth to the very heart of Guinée. As we are in community, each dependent on the other, so do we stand in relationship to the loa.

One does not take without giving, one does not give without taking. In all exchanges there is reciprocity, a sharing of benefit.

This section provides a context for the sacrifices indicated by the 22 Roads (Major Arcana) and sacrifices for the spirits of the vessels. An individual can sacrifice for many reasons. In terms of this deck, sacrifice to the loa, orisha, or process represented by a particular card is called for if, within the context of a reading, that card (1) occupies the position of an obstacle, (2) occupies the position of a particular strong point you wish to further strengthen, (3) occupies the position of a weak point you wish to strengthen, (4) shows that a particular loa or orisha wishes to be fed. The section on readings gives examples of particular layouts for the cards that can indicate these conditions.

It is not as important *what* is given as *how* it is given. We give what we can and in return receive immeasurable grace. In Haiti, the appetites of the loa are well defined; foods and manner of presentation are very exact. In their migration to New Orleans, the loa seem to have acquired a much more catholic appetite. With a bit of love for the loa as a sauce, a wide range of sacrifices is acceptable. As Akoko, a Voodoo practitioner and theorist, would say, "Even small efforts are greatly rewarded." In any sacrifice, sincerity is a major element. These things having been stated, let us build a Spirit House, an internal place within our hearts and souls from which to offer the external forms of sacrifice.

The word "sacrifice" is taken from the Latin *sacer* (sacred) and *facere* (to make). To sacrifice is to make sacred. This is an extremely important point and forms the foundation of the Spirit House in which we will make sacrifice.

That which is sacrificed is catapulted into the realm of the sacred. The duality of sacred as opposed to mundane underlying this statement does not indicate a hierarchical relationship. Sacredness is a state that appends itself to objects of the world. To deal in the mundane (*mundus*, the world) is to invite the influx of the sacred. In turn, in all that is sacred there is a yearning for the touch of the mundane. The path of the sacred and mundane circles in upon itself, forming a Gordian knot that mocks the naming or separation of its two strands.

Perhaps sacrifice, more than any other spiritual exercise, defines and encapsulates our Western culture's fall from grace. The common understanding of sacrifice is based on a "giving up." It is as if when something is made sacred (sacrificed) it is lost to us. This sense of loss defines our position, where we stand in relation to that which is sacred. It is as if we habitually stand outside the circle of the sacred. However, sacrifice need not connote separation. That which is given flares on the horizon, providing light for all. Its fires feed on both the sacred and the mundane. In the heart of the flames, the World burns. In the dancing tips of the flames does Spirit know its true measure; its ephemeral essence is given full range.

All of the sacrifices listed for the Roads are *mange sec* (dry meal), or without blood. This was done for a number of reasons, primarily the nature of the society in which we live. In general, we do not slaughter our own food. This, some believe, creates an unnatural situation where the shedding of blood takes on foreign and unnecessarily morbid implications. Life lives upon life. This obvious natural law seems to have become a secret hid within the butcher's shrink-wrap. If you do not kill the animals you eat, it is best to not even consider taking the life of an animal in order to feed the loa. All of us have ancestors who at one point offered animals in sacrifice and, I can guarantee you, they also killed and dressed the meat they themselves ate. To perform the former without the context of the latter is to court abuse of the ritual.

Personally, I would recommend killing and dressing your own food for a year before offering animal life in sacrifice. This would create a context for the sacrifice outside the mainstream culture's morbid fascination with blood and death.

The object of sacrifice can reflect your choice of sustenance. If you are a vegetarian, offer vegetables. If you are a fruitarian, offer fruits. The loa does not necessarily share your appetites, but there is a point at which your spirit will embrace that of the loa. If the means of your sacrifice are repugnant to you, your distaste will surely taint that which is given.

At this time in the United States, it may be that money constitutes the best sacrifice (conversation with Frater Turbator, 1992). Money is greatly cherished, and if that which is sacrificed is held in high esteem, great power will flow through the act. To sacrifice an amount of money to a loa and then distribute the money to the poor is an excellent sacrifice.

To conclude, here are a few points from my experience sacrificing to the loa: The loa always elicit a sacrifice, whether we choose its object or not. One reason to consciously offer sacrifice is to be in a position of choosing what is sacrificed. It makes no sense to "lose" three cymbals from a trap drum set when three pieces of brass, consciously offered, would have sufficed.

If you have sufficient power or connaissance, the sacrifice will come to you and make itself known. In my case, fruits and vegetables appropriate for sacrifice have a way of showing up when I need them.

The loa and our species walk hand in hand. As we change and evolve, so do the loa. There may come a time when we live on nothing but light. I would not be a bit surprised if the loa should follow suit.

To sacrifice is to create a channel cut deep into the earth, through which benefit flows both ways. To sacrifice is to give freely to the sacred, to move one's attention from acquisition to open-handed giving. Nature is said to abhor a vacuum; once the hand that gives is empty, it will soon be filled with the particular grace of the loa it has fed.

These are the planks I recommend you use to build a Spirit House to make sacrifice. The table that follows suggests appropriate objects for sacrifice to the loa, orisha, and processes represented by the cards of the Twenty-two Roads and the vessels. Trust your intuition; the loa will tell you what they want. If you feel uncomfortable or sense even a hint of coercion, give thanks and close the reading. For further guidance, see the section "On Using These Cards."

APPROPRIATE MATERIALS FOR SACRIFICE

TWENTY-TWO ROADS

Aleph 0
Sacrifice: .

Damballah and Ayida's World Egg
Egg atop a mound of white cornmeal (traditional)
Grenadine (traditional)

Beth I
Sacrifice:

Dr. John
A drum; the playing of a drum

Gimel II
Sacrifice:

Marie Laveau
Salt water (as derived from the reading of her name, explained in the card's text)

Daleth III
Sacrifice:

Ayizan
Palm fringe; mountain rocks

Tzaddi IV
Sacrifice:

Loco
Green herbs (traditional)

Vav V
Sacrifice

Master of the Head
Burn a bit of your hair

Zayin VI
Sacrifice:

Marassa
Candy, sweets (traditional)
Grilled corn (traditional)

Cheth VII
Sacrifice:

Dance
Sweat produced by dancing

Teth VIII (XI)
Sacrifice:

Possession
Skin oils from the back of your neck; this is
where the spirits enter and leave

Yod IX
Sacrifice:

Couché
Frayed palm leaves

Kaph X
Sacrifice:

The Market
Produce found on the street of a market or
discarded produce from a market; purchased
produce if discarded or found material is not
available

Lamed XI (VIII)
Sacrifice:

Secret Societies
Milk and/or meat of a coconut

Mem XII
Sacrifice:

Zombi
On a piece of paper, write a statement about
which you feel strongly, a statement you would
live by, defend; burn the paper, offering the
light and heat to invigorate the Zombi

Nun XIII
Sacrifice:

Les Morts
Flowers of jasmine or wisteria
Alcohol (traditional)

Samekh XIV
Sacrifice:

Ti Bon Ange
A product of one's works and labors

Ayin XV
Sacrifice:

Courir Le Mardi Gras
Alcohol to heat up the Ride
A rope tied in a knot to contain the energies of the Ride

Pe XVI
Sacrifice:

Deluge
River water

Hé XVII
Sacrifice:

Z'Étoile
A material symbol (such as a contract or birth certificate) of your acceptance of an unavoidable or irrevocable event; a flower, in that flowers are stars of the earth

Qoph XVIII
Sacrifice:

Magick Mirror
A mirror

Resh XIX
Sacrifice:

Gros Bon Ange
A material symbol of one's self

Shin XX
Sacrifice:

Ancestors
Alcohol (traditional)
Coffee (traditional)
Food, drink, or objects liked by particular ancestors

Tau XXI
Sacrifice:

Carnival
Bright cloth, beads

Wild Card
Sacrifice:

Les Barons
Rum (traditional)

THE VESSELS

1: Kether

Damballah La Flambeau
Sacrifice: An egg placed on a mound of hot peppers

Ayida Wedo
Sacrifice: An egg in the colors of the rainbow

Damballah Wedo
Sacrifice: An egg placed on a mound of flour or sea sand; cabbage (traditional)

Olodumare
Sacrifice: A material symbol of your highest aspirations

2: Chokmah

Nan Nan Bouclou La Flambeau
Sacrifice: Medicinal herbs mixed with a pungent infusion

Gran Ibo
Sacrifice: Leaves of swamp plants (take care not to kill the plant)

Nan Nan Bouclou
Sacrifice: Medicinal herbs

Olofi
Sacrifice: A manifestation of your creativity

3: Binah

Guedeh La Flambeau
Sacrifice: Rum in which hot peppers soak

Manman Brigitte
Sacrifice: Nettle (traditional); rocks from a cemetery

Guedeh
Sacrifice: Rum and cigars (traditional)

Oyá
Sacrifice: Dust from a graveyard, eggplant (traditional); do *not* offer Yemayá sacrifices along with Oyá (traditional)

4: Chesed

Agwé La Flambeau
Sacrifice: Small raft covered with hot and spicy foods

La Baleine
Sacrifice: Seawater

Agwé
Sacrifice: Small raft covered with foods for a feast (traditional)

Obatalá
Sacrifice: White substances and materials; no wine, especially no palm wine (traditional)

5: Geburah

Ogoun La Flambeau
Sacrifice: Iron dusted with gunpowder

Ogoun Bhalin'dio
Sacrifice: Bits of iron in seawater

Ogoun Ferraille
Sacrifice: Iron or any metal that can be worked at the forge (traditional)

Oggún
Sacrifice: Iron or any metal; roots, nuts (traditional)

6: Tiphereth

Legba La Flambeau
Sacrifice: Pipe tobacco soaked in hot chili oil

Shi-Li-Bo Nouvavou
Sacrifice: Stream or pond water

Dan-i
Sacrifice: White substances and white foods

Legba
Sacrifice: Pipe tobacco (traditional)

Elegguá
Sacrifice: Candy, sweets, fruits, toys, rum, cigars (traditional)

7: Netzach

Erzulie La Flambeau
Sacrifice: Jewelry dusted with gunpowder

La Sirène
Sacrifice: Sing to her; pearls

Erzulie Freda Dahomey
Sacrifice: Perfume; French pastry; pearls or jewels (traditional)

Oshún
Sacrifice: Honey, oranges, or eggs (taste the honey in her presence: she was once offered poisoned honey); gold is liked by her (traditional)

8: Hod

Simbi La Flambeau
Sacrifice: Yams seasoned with hot pepper

Simbi d'l'eau
Sacrifice: Stream water

Simbi
Sacrifice: Yams (traditional)

Shangó
Sacrifice: Apples, bananas (traditional)

9: Yesod

Masa La Flambeau
Sacrifice: Well water containing hot peppers

Madame La Lune
Sacrifice: Pale or white seashells

Masa
Sacrifice: Well water

Yemayá
Sacrifice: Coconut balls, sugar cane syrup, melons (traditional); do *not* feed with Oyá (traditional)

10: Malkuth

Azaka La Flambeau
Sacrifice: Millet cake, ear of corn sprinkled with hot sauce

Gran Bois
Sacrifice: Leaves (traditional)

Azaka
Sacrifice: Millet cake, ear of corn (traditional)

Ochosi
Sacrifice: Fruit, candy, a drink made of milk, honey, and cornmeal (traditional)

POSSESSION

Possession, the process indicated by the eighth Road of this Tarot, is possibly the most dramatic manifestation of the loa and, to the new-world mind, the most fearsome aspect of Voodoo. However, it is good to remember that possession is not an all-or-nothing phenomenon. It can make itself known through localized body movements, such as the sudden stiffening of an arm or jerking of a foot during ritual, strong and persistent shaking, unusual head movements, or the overpowering desire to perform a meaningless (in a conscious sense) action. All of these motions can be related to a partial possession by the loa, called for in the context of a rite. While not as intense as total possession, partial possession can serve as a valuable avenue through which the spirits can communicate their wishes and wisdom. It is generally unwise to court total possession without the assistance of an experienced practitioner (see "On Using These Cards," p. 32).

The real issue in our culture is not possession by loa, demons, or angels, but possession by what is commonly known as personality, the cluster of traits that we identify as ourselves and that we project in the world around us. Personality is such an acceptable and pervasive expression of self in our society that it is frequently mistaken for self. To the extent that we identify with the roles, mores, and expectations of our personalities they possess us, strangling the vast array of possibilities inherent in self. Ritual possession is one way of breaking free from the confines of a too deeply entrenched personality.

Possession is most alarming if we view ourselves as static, fixed entities with an inborn mandate to resist all but superficial change. According to this view, *self* is an object. The self is placed within the same category as a car or a house, as something we own. It is frightening to consider the possibility of a force taking our house away; in the same manner it is frightening to consider the loss of self. Self is seen as an unchanging thing that we as beings possess.

An alternative perspective views *self* as a process. Seen in this way, the self has an ephemeral quality and is always changing. The "mask of the self" (conversation with Nema, ca. 1973) is at best momentary. I have photographs of myself as a child, but I am no longer that self. I have memories of myself before I sat down to type, but I am no longer that self. One being can wear any number of "masks" or "selves." It has been said that the one constant of existence is change. The phenomenon of possession is not a special case; it is an extreme point on the continuum of constant change.

According to the situation, some selves are more appropriate or convenient than others. Possession is in part characterized by sudden change in the visible attributes of self: language, mannerisms, memories, appearance, and so on. Such a change might prove inconvenient while trying to cash a check in a bank, but it would be entirely appropriate in a ritual space that has been constructed in a manner conducive to the change.

While ritual possession certainly allows us to see the limits of personality, there are three distinct viewpoints on the role personality plays in possession. The first holds that the strength or weakness of one's personality is irrelevant; when the loa come, they have the power to pass through the strongest of barriers and the ability to mount the weakest of personalities. The second viewpoint is that a lack of personality is preferable; one should strive to let go of personality and become a clear channel through which the Mysteries can speak. A third view holds that a personality must be present in the practitioner for the process of possession to take hold. If he or she is a clear channel, the spirits move on through; there is nothing for them to grasp. An ego or something akin to it is necessary for the spirits to rub against in order to create the friction and heat that allows them to solidify in possession. The Mysteries solidify around the practitioner's ego; the stronger the ego, the more tenacious the possession (conversation with Mishlen Linden, 1992).

Within the Christian world view, possession is almost always indulged in by demonic forces. For those raised as Christians (with the exception of those denominations where speaking in tongues and being taken by the Spirit are common), accepting possession as a valid expression of the religious impulse will require some deep unlearning of very early indoctrination. Perhaps "taken by the spirit" serves as a better descriptor than "possession."

In using this Tarot, the type of possession that focuses on the hands may be the most valuable (see "Readings," p. 232). Giving the loa access to your hands as they choose cards during readings is a powerful technique. Mishlen Linden writes, "The palm . . . is also that part of ourselves most easily possessed. Consider automatic writing, or great art. While we may be afraid to let the Other take our minds, we rest easier in allowing it temporary use of the hands" (1991, p. 21). It is possible to engage in the process of possession by degrees; have faith in Those that guide you.

THE VÈVÈ

Every loa has its own vèvè, or ritual drawing, which a Voodoo practitioner will use to summon the power of that loa. The vèvès and other ritual drawings appear with the text describing each card. The vèvè represents a path that can be traveled by both the loa and the practitioner. It traverses the edge of things; it is literally a path off the edge of the earth into the Waters. The great spiritual forces that live in the Waters can follow this path to the physical space occupied by the ritual and the practitioner. Some loa are so vast and swollen with the power of new and ancient services that they can make the journey to physical space without the active call of the practitioner. The mere physical presence of their vèvè inscribed on the earth can be enough to allow for their sure passage.

Vèvès are usually drawn on the open ground using cornmeal. Their artistry and power in part arises from the fact that, like life, they are not exact. The thickness of the lines and the spatial relationship of their elements change, as does the earth on which they are most often drawn.

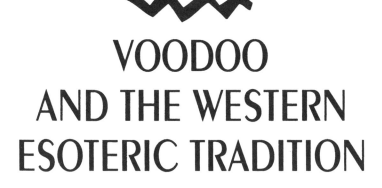

VOODOO
AND THE WESTERN
ESOTERIC TRADITION

VOODOO AND THE TREE OF LIFE

All great religious systems of the world demonstrate a marked degree of commonality. A good many of the practitioners of Western occultism are familiar with the Hebraic glyph of the Tree of Life as it has been filtered through the Golden Dawn; therefore, *The New Orleans Voodoo Tarot* uses the Tree as a fundamental structure upon which to "hang" the cards.

The Tree of Life as it is commonly pictured in esoteric circles was first published in Kircher's *Oedipus Aegypticus* in 1652. The development of the design has a lengthy history and "its historical roots appear buried in the secret past of Mystery religions" (Wang, 1983, p. 30). The Tree is deeply associated with Hebraic mysticism or Kabala, a word which can be translated "to receive," as in reception of knowledge from the Divine. Two works that formulated and gave life to the Tree are the Sepher Yetzirah (The Book of Formation), dating from between the third and sixth centuries A.D. by an unknown author; and the Zohar (Book of Splendor), committed to writing about 1280 A.D. by

Moses de Leon (or, as stated in the Zohar itself, by Rabbi Shimon ben Yohi and his son Rabbi El'azar while they spent thirteen years in a cave to escape Roman persecution around the second century A.D.). The dates and names are important but, like the Tarot itself, the glyph and the doctrine may reach immeasurably farther back in time.

The original Golden Dawn is an esoteric society that was located in England from about 1888 to 1914. During these short years it changed the landscape of Western occultism. It popularized the type of Kabalism that today is associated with a wide range of Western esoteric societies such as the O.T.O. (Ordo Templi Orientis), E.O.D. (Esoteric Order of Dagon), B.C. (Bate Cabal), and TOPY (Temple of Psychick Youth); its members, specifically MacGregor Mathers, A. E. Waite, and Aleister Crowley, provided the commonly used attributions of the Tarot cards to the Tree of Life.

As a representation of the eternal, the Tree of Life has such potency that the occultist Frater Achad described it as the anatomy of the body of God. Aleister Crowley's book, 777, uses the Tree of Life as a basic grid in comparing numerous mystical and religious systems. The esoteric and practical perfection of the Tree makes it a valuable tool in the unfolding of Voodoo to the Western mind. The graphic nature of the vessels and paths of the Tree point to connections between the loa that otherwise can go unnoticed. Community is all-important in Voodoo, and the Tree of Life shows the living spirit of community that exists between the loa, the rites, and the congregation. The bibliography lists books that can be of great help in the study of the Tree of Life and Kabala. Among the forefront are *The Qabalistic Tarot* by Robert Wang, *Magick High and Low* by Oneida Toups, and *The Complete Golden Dawn System of Magick* by Israel Regardie. The "Readings" section of this book gives a Tarot reading which uses the Tree of Life.

The diagram of the Tree of Life following this section illustrates the 10 vessels (circles), which serve to hold particular aspects of the Creator's grace (see the Tree of Life reading, p. 241), and the 22 paths which connect the vessels and have attributes of their own derived from the Hebrew letter that the path represents. The cards attributed to the vessels and the paths are indicated. A primary loa and orisha is given for each of the vessels. Daath, the eleventh "nonexistent" vessel, is shown as the home of the trickster Barons. The four levels of manifestation—archetypal, creative, formative, and active—are indicated on the left of the diagram. These levels trace the type of action manifested by the flow of grace or aché as it moves from Kether (1) to Malkuth (10). The traditional Western name of the card is included for comparison with the Voodoo Tarot name.

At first glance this diagram looks very complex, but with a few hours of study and meditation, the Tree will begin to show a divine and forthright simplicity. If you are versed in Western kabalistic mysticism, this diagram will allow for rapid understanding of this deck.

Ninety-three is a number of great significance to the Thelemic community. Numerologically, 93 is the number of the Greek words thelema (will) and agapé (love) (Crowley, 1929–30, p. 260). Will and love are key words of the Thelemic Gnosis as described by Crowley. There is at present a good deal of interest in Voodoo on the part of those who work within the Thelemic and other primarily Western esoteric traditions. The letters of the three crosspaths of the Tree add up to 93 (conversation with Mishlen Linden, 1989). It may be of use to those who follow the paths of both Thelema and Voodoo to make special note of the cards attributed to these crosspaths in the present deck.

Hebrew Letter (& translation)	Number	Thelemic Card	Voodoo Card
Daleth (Door)	4	Empress	Ayizan
Teth (Serpent)	9	Lust	Possession
Pé (Mouth)	80	Tower	Deluge

These crosspaths are like rungs of a ladder one may use in climbing the Tree to greater understanding.

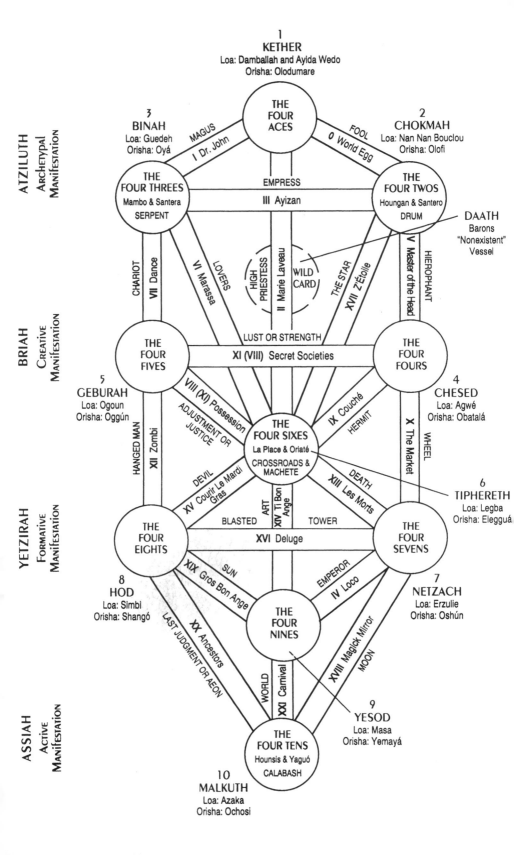

It is also interesting to note that in Gematria, the number of the Voodoo Marassa, or Divine Twins, is the same as the Hebrew word for "two."

Marassa: M (40) + R (200) + S (60) + S (60) = 360
Two: Shin (300) + Nun (50) + Yodh (10) = 360

Voodoo has always grown through contact with other religious traditions. This trend continues and seems to be very active through contacts with Thelemic and earth-based traditions. However, in the march to common understandings, individual differences can sometimes be caught underfoot and flattened. If the powers and scope of the loa have been altered through this use of the Tree, or if the Tree has been—gently or otherwise—twisted beyond its proper form, we hope that the creation of common accords in some way balances the damage.

TAROT AND VOODOO

Tarot is a tool used for divination and deep contact with spiritual forces. The Tarot is usually a deck of 22 picture cards (Trumps), 40 cards (Pips) divided equally into the four suits or elements, and 16 Court Cards. The Trumps are numbered from 0 to 21. They begin with 0 to show that the card thus designated represents the beginning of all things from nothing, and are attributed to the 22 letters of the Hebrew alphabet. The Pip cards are numbered from 1 to 10. The Court cards are composed of four Kings (or Knights), four Queens, four Princes, and four Princesses. All of these cards are assigned specific divinatory meanings and contemplative functions.

The New Orleans Voodoo Tarot has taken these meanings and found or evolved a more or less parallel meaning within the context of Voodoo. A reader need not know the use and meanings of the traditional Western Tarot deck, but if he or she does, this knowledge can for the most part be applied to the Voodoo Tarot. A major difference between the New Orleans Voodoo Tarot and traditional Tarots is that the element Earth is in no way seen as inferior to the other elements.

In the New Orleans Voodoo Tarot, the 22 picture cards or Trumps are called "Roads" (a Wild Card is included to bring the number of picture cards to 23), the 40 Pip cards are called "Spirits," and the 16 Court Cards are called "Temple Cards."

The New Orleans Voodoo Tarot uses the form of Tetragrammaton, with its elemental attributions of fire, water, air, and earth, to provide a structure for the Spirit and Temple cards. This is the form used by most traditional Tarot decks. Tetragrammaton literally means "four letters" and is used to designate the four consonants of the ancient Hebrew name for God, which was considered too sacred to pronounce. The Hebrew letters are *yod, hé, vav, hé,* which in English correspond to the letters JHVH. The more modern spoken pronunciation is Jehovah.

This name with its four letters moved from its Jewish origin into the general stream of Western mysticism and occult practice. Within Western mysticism, the letters of Tetragrammaton are used to symbolize the power of the Creator as it moves through the four elements: *yod* is fire, the first *hé* is water, *vav* is air, and the second *hé* is earth. These elements are both symbolic and real and refer to whole categories of more or less arbitrary associations.

This Tarot makes use of four nations, or Voodoo traditions, that roughly correspond to the four elements of Western tradition, fire, water, air, and earth. Nations refer to a grouping of rites and spirits that walk together and are related by common origin or theme.

The first of these nations is Petro, a form of worship common in Haiti, which corresponds to fire. La Flambeau rites are also associated with the element of fire. These rites tend toward the revolutionary in that their "fiery" content challenges the established order of things. For example, the Petro ritual of Bois Caiman, performed on August 14, 1791, began the Haitian War of Independence. In this rite, those present took an oath to follow the houngan (priest) Boukman in a fight for independence. The war ended in 1804, and Haiti emerged as the second independent country in the western hemisphere. The name "La Flambeau" is taken from the torch carriers who light the way for nighttime carnival parades. Carnival literally means "farewell to flesh," and it is within the heat of carnival that the "flesh," or the established order of things, is upset and transcended.

The rites of the Congo nation, the second represented here, according to Milo Rigaud (1969, p. 72), are attributed to the element of water. These rites and the loa they summon are in general of a more jarring character than the Rada, or air rites, yet not so jarring as the Petro rites. This follows the elemental attributions in that air is the least harsh element, then comes water and then fire (Santería, the earthy nation of this deck, is a system in itself, independent of Voodoo, and will be treated as such).

Fresh water is the precious element of Voodoo. Water is commonly used to assist the loa in entering ritual space; they are said to walk the "water road." Streams that well up from the earth are sacred places where the voices of the loa or spirits can be heard. In this Tarot, the Congo nation is attributed to water in order to pay homage to a sacred site in New Orleans, Congo Square. It is a place of grace, where Dr. John drummed and Marie Laveau danced and presided over the sometimes legal dances of the enslaved people of the city. It is now the site of drum groups and numerous black cultural events. As the water road of the loa winds its way through New Orleans, it flows close to the surface in Congo Square.

The third of these nations is Rada, which in terms of this Tarot corresponds to air. The Rada rites are characterized by a formal, subtle quality. They claim origin from the rites performed in the well-established traditional kingdom of Dahomey, with its highly developed religious structures. The Rada is attributed to air in that Western occultism postulates a connection between air and the intellect. The intellect is seen as airy in its flights of imagination and its quick rush of thoughts, one tumbling over the other. Within the context of the Rada rites, the intellect is not the child of illusion but a liberating force—a force useful in the forging of connections, a force that can be used to clothe spirit in a cloak of many colors.

Santería is a sister religion to Voodoo. In deference to its power and influence in the New World it is used in this Tarot as the nation that resonates well with the element earth. Solidity, strength, and the ability to take hold of the conditions at hand and grow are attributes of the element earth. Santería, with its tremendous growth and following in the New World, has definitely managed to successfully bring its high spiritual teachings to the sphere of the element earth.

Santería and the spirits and practices that have come to be called Voodoo find their initial theology in different African peoples. Santería derives a good deal of its heritage from the religious practices of the Yoruba people of Nigeria. Voodoo looks to the Fon-speaking people of the once-great Dahomey as a major source, with contributions from the Ibo, Congo, Nagos, and other African peoples. The families of spirits of these African peoples, though related, are different. As Courlander writes, "Africa was a continent of many cultures and nations, and its belief systems varied . . . even neighboring peoples such as the Ibos, the Yorubas, and the Mahis did not have common religious traditions" (Courlander, 1960, p. 8).

Santería has developed a strong and elaborate ceremonial structure firmly connected to a widely recognized hierarchy. The Voodoo of New Orleans is individual in tone and in most cases chronicles one person's or a group's relationship with the spirits. The traditions which were to become Voodoo emphasized religion as a family affair. The head of the family would often act as the liaison between the family and the spirits. The Voodoo of New Orleans in many ways mirrors this method of working. While this is a Voodoo Tarot and the rituals and processes are Voodoo in nature, it would be disrespectful not to include the names and some information concerning the great orishas, spirits of Santería, in the cards and text.

The following table brings together elements of the deck that are scattered throughout the book. If you wish to begin reading with the cards immediately and are familiar with traditional Tarot, the table should provide sufficient information for most divinatory purposes. It also highlights the many parallels—and some differences—between this deck and the traditional Western Tarot decks.

NEW ORLEANS VOODOO TAROT

TWENTY-TWO ROADS & THE WILD CARD*

Aleph 0	The Fool	Damballah and Ayida's World Egg
Beth I	The Magus	Dr. John
Gimel II	High Priestess	Marie Laveau
Daleth III	The Empress	Ayizan
Tzaddi IV	The Emperor	Loco
Vav V	The Hierophant	Master of the Head
Zayin VI	The Lovers	Marassa
Cheth VII	The Chariot	Dance
Teth VIII (XI)	Strength/Lust	Possession
Yod IX	Hermit	Couché
Kaph X	Wheel	The Market
Lamed XI (VIII)	Justice/Adjustment	Secret Societies
Mem XII	Hanged Man	Zombi
Nun XIII	Death	Les Morts
Samekh XIV	Temperance/Art	Ti Bon Ange
Ayin XV	The Devil	Courir Le Mardi Gras
Pé XVI	Blasted Tower	Deluge

*The arrangement given here generally follows the Thoth Tarot of Frieda Harris and Aleister Crowley. The numeration of the cards begins with 0, the VIIIth and XIth cards can exchange places in order to maintain zodiacal rhythm (Crowley, 1971, p. 9), and the IVth and XVIIth Hebrew letters with their attendant cards do change positions in response to the shift from the Aeon of Pisces to the Aeon of Aquarius or Horus.

Hé XVII	The Star	Z'Étoile
Qoph XVIII	The Moon	Magick Mirror
Resh XIX	The Sun	Gros Bon Ange
Shin XX	Last Judgment/Aeon	Ancestors
Tau XXI	The World	Carnival
Wild Card		Les Barons

FORTY SPIRITS

Element	Fire	Water	Air	Earth
Letter of Tetragrammaton:	Yod	Hé	Vav	Hé
Nation/ Tradition:	Petro	Congo	Rada	Santería
Vessels: 1 Kether:	Damballah La Flambeau	Ayida Wedo	Damballah Wedo	Olodumare
2 Chokmah:	Nan Nan Bouclou La Flambeau	Gran Ibo	Nan Nan Bouclou	Olofi
3 Binah:	Guedeh La Flambeau	Manman Brigitte	Guedeh	Oyá
4 Chesed:	Agwé La Flambeau	La Baleine*	Agwé	Obatalá
5 Geburah:	Ogoun La Flambeau	Ogoun Bhalin'dio*	Ogoun Ferraille	Oggún

* *Baleine* and *Bhalin'dio* both refer to the whale. *Baleine* reflects a standard French spelling, while *Bhalin'dio* is a variant. The Creole used in the Voodoo of New Orleans and spoken in Haiti is not strictly codified as a written language. West African linguistic constraints,

Element	Fire	Water	Air	Earth
6 Tiphereth:	Legba La Flambeau	Shi-Li-Bo Nouvavou and Dan-i	Legba	Elegguá
7 Netzach:	Erzulie La Flambeau	La Sirène	Erzulie Freda Dahomey	Oshún
8 Hod:	Simbi La Flambeau	Simbi d'l'eau	Simbi	Shangó
9 Yesod:	Masa La Flambeau	Madame La Lune	Masa	Yemayá
10 Malkuth:	Azaka La Flambeau	Gran Bois	Azaka	Ochosi

SIXTEEN TEMPLE CARDS

Drum: (King/Wand)	Houngan	Houngan	Houngan	Santero
Serpent: (Queen/Cup)	Mambo	Mambo	Mambo	Santera
Crossroads & Machete: (Prince/Sword)	La Place	La Place	La Place	Oriaté
Calabash: (Princess/ Pentacle)	Hounsis	Hounsis	Hounsis	Yaguó

French, English, and Spanish mix to produce a variety of spellings for the same word. The orthography used in this book reflects the spellings most commonly used by Milo Rigaud and Maya Deren. Both Rigaud and Deren are individuals whose authority is widely recognized by practitioners of Voodoo. *The Haitian Creole–English–French Dictionary* (Valdman, 1981) provides an official orthography which does not seem to be widely recognized by voodooists.

ON USING THESE CARDS

The most important message of this section is not so much a warning as an injunction. Learn to trust in yourself and your own intuitions; what you are is larger than the mind in its everyday workings can ever enfold. If, in the course of a reading or making sacrifice, you feel uncomfortable with a practice, process, or loa, give thanks, sacrifice, and quickly leave the situation. If a loa asks something of you that you are not comfortable giving, give thanks to that loa for the contact, perform a sacrifice, and leave the situation.

There is within all of us connaissance. It may be present to a greater or lesser degree, but it is there. Connaissance has been described as intuition, a sense of things, an internal knowing without external support, or a marriage of the intellect with wild and direct experience outside the realm of meaningful verbal description. This knowing carries within it the voice of our deepest self, the voice that is always in contact with the loa.

Whatever name you give it, connaissance is something to be trusted. If something feels or seems incorrect to you, if there is a sense of wrongness connected to any contact with the loa—or, for that matter, any spiritual force—then it is best to move away from that contact; something is amiss.

If you have the sense that some practice is not right for you or that some type of contact with the spirits is to be avoided without being able to identify a definite reason that explains and justifies the feeling, then I would definitely recommend that you back away from that practice or contact. The inability to find a reason for your uneasiness may show that it comes from levels beyond the conscious mind. There is in all of us a deep sense of what is right for us, a deep sense of the role we play in the unfolding of the universe. We know, inexplicably yet in no uncertain terms, when our actions or involvements violate our inner core.

Once you have reached the spirits, they may propose various courses of action. Some suggestions are practical in nature; for example, you may be told of an object that can be kept in a car to avoid accidents. Or, on the more esoteric side, you may be told by a loa that he or she wishes to marry you. Feel free in all ways to decline. Offer sacrifice and back off. In the event things become more than you can or wish to handle, there are excellent contacts for ritual work in the "Contacts & Supplies" section. Involvement in total possession is another example of a type of contact with the loa that would most probably be safest in the presence of a priest or priestess.

It is extremely important to always keep your word when you deal with the loa. If you say that you are going to something, be sure that you do it. There is little room for explanation or reprieve. My experience with the loa is that while they are generous in the bestowal of benefits, they are exact in holding the voodooist to his or her word.

The deck can be used for malevolent Workings. What constitutes malevolence is best decided between the voodooist and Bon Dieu Bon (the Great, Good Spirit). While there is little value in pursuing such an individualized topic here, it may be of benefit to remember that actions tend to return to their source. The means of approaching the question of evil that I like began with the thinking of Saint Augustine. He argued that evil consisted in choosing the lesser of two goods. This statement is certainly problematic, but if indeed you do have a singular place in the community and a unique mission to fulfill, any action that pulls you from that mission—even if that action is commonly regarded as good—is the lesser of two goods, and therefore evil.

When you observe or participate in a Voodoo ceremony, do not judge it by the information given in any book. Voodoo is extremely individualized, and New Orleans Voodoo is among the most idiosyncratic. In fact, if you do not get a good deal of variance there is a definite possibility that what you are watching or participating in is more of a show based upon what someone thinks you want—or would pay—to see.

One of the most important cautions and injunctions concerns the ancestors. The importance of your relationship with the ancestors can not be overstated. Remember them and they will remember you. Forget or neglect them and their distress will hang like a millstone around your neck. A good way of honoring the ancestors is the rite repeated on page 110. The sincere performance of this rite or something like it will be your greatest assurance of success in Voodoo.

It has been said that most often an individual is chosen to work with the Voodoo. One does not choose. But this is a really moot point in that being chosen often takes into account the desire to take up the work. It is true that at times the loa call strongly and a person, for one reason or another, resists the call. The loa can then act to make that person's life very complicated. If you believe that you are involved in a situation like this, get in touch with a priest or priestess listed in the "Contacts & Supplies" section at the back of the book. You may be able to benefit from their specialized and highly trained expertise.

If over time you feel uncomfortable with using these cards, it may help to remember that Voodoo is not for everyone—no spiritual system that I have had contact with can speak to all people in all places. There are many paths to the same goal and, for that matter, many types of Tarot that can be used in your readings.

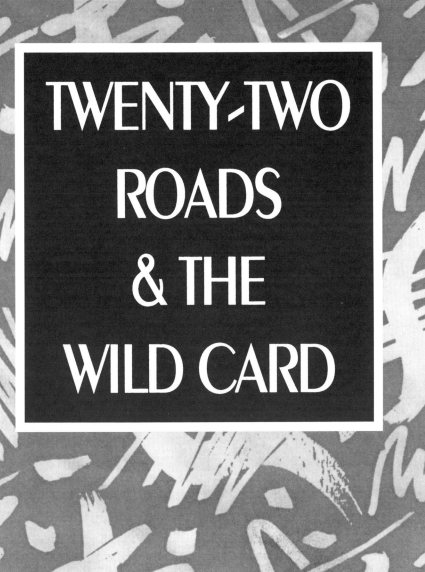

TWENTY-TWO
ROADS
& THE
WILD CARD

0

WORLD EGG

(BEGINNINGS • THE FOOL)

A point of power bursts forth from the waters of undifferentiated possibility. Ayida Wedo has given birth! From the vast chambers of the void, the egg (representing directed or focused possibility) is carried and warmed by Damballah Wedo. Cold space retreats at the contraction of his coils. The Will to Be has dared to manifest.

Ayida Wedo and Damballah Wedo are the holy serpents of Voodoo. Ayida Wedo is the female, and Damballah is the male. Like the serpents on the physician's caduceus, this pair of serpents brings change and the creation of new possibility.

Oswan Chamani, an Obi Man (a Jamaican priest of the Mysteries), once startled me by saying that the beginnings of religion lie in the mystery of birth, not in the mystery of death. Western anthropological thought generally holds that the impulse toward religion arose as a way of understanding death. The words of the Obi Man point to the ancient and beautiful mystery of birth, through which Spirit first showed itself to our species.

The World Egg forms the center of the Crossroads, the point from which all creation takes its measure. Though night rains come to wash out the far-reaching roads, still the central point remains. It is interesting to note that the Hebrew word for world, *Olam*, captures the sense of this card completely in that *Olam* also means "eternity." The World Egg, embodying the leap from nonbeing to being, is eternally present as the first step of all that would manifest.

This card shows the Great Snake coiled within the fastness of the void, holding the World Egg within its mouth. Birth has taken place, and the egg is protected and carried by the mouth of the snake. This refers to the creative powers of the Word. The Word, or rhythmic sound, defines and thus shapes the World.

Attributes of this card represent a fierce bursting forth of creative currents.

CONTEMPLATION

First manifestation of focused possibility, zero as the nothingness necessary for creation. This "0" as the issue of God the Mother, Ayida Wedo, and God the Father, Damballah Wedo.

DIVINATION

Surprise; the unexpected; beginnings; influence from the Highest in spiritual matters; possible disruption of physical matters.

DR. JOHN
(CRAFT • THE MAGUS)

Dr. John is a New Orleans personage who is traveling the starry road to the position of loa. He was a practitioner and sacred drummer of high renown in the city during the early 1800s. His aspect is that of a fierce, free African whose face was said to be tattooed with red and blue lines in the form of snakes. His virtues are those of a traditionalist dedicated to the maintenance of the strict African forms within Voodoo and those vibratory laws that govern the rhythms used to call the loa. The Spirit of the first Dr. John resides close to Congo Square in St. Louis Cemetery No. 1.

Dr. John still plays his drum in New Orleans and in the many parts of the New World alive with African rhythms. Listen. Late at night, the drumming never stops—now loud, now very, very soft. His is the power of sound. In the beginning was the Sound, the Word, the Rhythm. This is the pulsing road the spirits travel. The baton carried by the winged god Mercury was a rod of communication, of messages; Dr. John's baton becomes a drumstick with which he drums this world into existence and creates the link with the Invisibles.

His ability to bring power into the Voodoo rites is always harnessed, used in service to and at the word of the congregation or its leader, generally a priestess. His task was to produce bursts of energy from the drums on demand; the lines tattooed on his face helped him to channel the necessary power. A primary role of the ritual drummer is to provide rhythmic fuel to heat up a rite. It is an office of service to those assembled for the rite and requires great sensitivity to spoken as well as subtle injunctions. The ego that remained within him must often have chafed at this control, as his ability to raise power upon command was exercised to the point of bone-weariness.

There have been many Dr. Johns, which attests to the power the original Doctor was able to conjure and hold. After the first Doctor's death another Dr. John, who resembled the original closely, was quick to make his way into Voodoo circles.

The present Dr. John is a powerful musician whose music and stage presence have a strong Voodoo feel. He is greatly respected for his willingness to play benefits for worthy civic causes.

The aspect of this card is that of an intense drummer sitting astride his drum. One hand is raised and one is lowered in his playing, suggesting the essential unity of the worlds, "As above, so below." The scene for the card is Congo Square in New Orleans; the good Doctor is playing for one of the dances presided over by Marie Laveau. Congo Square was the officially sanctioned location for ritualized dancing by enslaved Africans in the early nineteenth century and is a holy site of great spiritual energy.

Attributes or powers attributed to this card include the use of rhythm to call the spiritual into the Visible World. Dr. John is a great patron of ritual drummers.

CONTEMPLATION

Rhythm . . . the pulsing of sound and silence . . . the extension and contraction of the Great Snake, giving rise to creation.

DIVINATION

Craft; consummate skill in the matter at hand; occult powers or wisdom; ability to see root causes clearly; identification of the individual Will with a greater or more inclusive Will.

MARIE LAVEAU
(CONNECTION • HIGH PRIESTESS)

Marie Laveau is, along with the good Doctor, moving into the position of loa. Her occult skills, ability to connect peoples of diverse interest, and great works of charity are at the forefront of those qualities time and remembrance have distilled from the matrix of her life. Her "small house" in St. Louis Cemetery No. 1 is well supplied with flowers and other offerings.

Marie Laveau, also called "Madame L.," lived in New Orleans from 1794 to 1881. She probably traveled no more than 20 miles from the city during her lifetime, but at the present time her fame has spread well beyond the Americas. Rose, a priestess who presently lives in New Orleans, holds Marie Laveau to be the last of the great Voodoo

Queens, but she says that another may come to fill that role. The stature Marie Laveau enjoys has certainly not been reached by any other voodooist to date. The power of her work has changed both the internal and external expressions of Voodoo in the United States.

She presided at the Voodoo rites of St. John's Eve and the dances on Congo Square. Through her abilities to influence the authorities, Voodoo became a somewhat tolerated, if not acceptable, form of religious expression. During the great yellow fever epidemics that swept through New Orleans in 1832 and 1853, she was tireless and selfless in her care for the victims. When she died (on June 16, 1881), the *Daily Picayune*, a major New Orleans paper, ran the following as a part of an editorial:

> All in all Marie Laveau was a wonderful woman. Doing good for the sake of doing good alone, she obtained no reward, ofttimes meeting with prejudice and loathing; she was nevertheless contented and did not lag in her work. She had the cause of the people at heart and was with them in everything. . . . Marie's name will not be forgotten in New Orleans.

Marie Laveau's name will not be forgotten in any city where the spirits of Voodoo are honored.

The aspect of Marie Laveau shown by this card emphasizes gate-keeping and connection. Her strong face looks straight out at the reader as she parts a curtain of cowrie shells. She offers entrance, a look beyond the veil—but only if one can meet and reflect her steady gaze.

An interpretation of the very name Marie Laveau points the way toward those attributes that survived her person and continue to live to this day. Marie finds its root in the Hebrew word *mar*, which refers to the bitterness, the salt, of seawater. In French, *lav* means "wash," and *eau* means "liquid." The name forms an admirable glyph of the great waters and their ability to return all who approach to a state of pristine ritual purity, fit and inviting for the in-dwelling of the Spirits.

CONTEMPLATION

The Great Waters as the beginning and end of existence. In these Waters, purity of purpose is restored and connection to the Spirit is strengthened.

DIVINATION

Connection is possible between seemingly diverse elements. The words of Aleister Crowley speak most elegantly of Our Lady: "Pure, exalted and gracious influence enters the matter. Hence change, alteration, increase and decrease, fluctuation" (Book of Thoth).

AYIZAN

(LOVE • THE EMPRESS)

Ayizan is a most ancient loa. She is a patron of the ritual purity of the hounfor, the Voodoo place of worship. Her emblem is the frayed palm branch, which is a symbol of purity. By purity here is meant such qualities as clearness of mission and focus of devotion, not a simple holding back from experience. The frayed palm may be understood as a mask or filter through which the new initiate perceives the world. Each new initiation implies a new vision of the world, a new filter or mask. It is said that there are three births: the birth into the Visible World, the birth provided by initiation, and the birth that comes when one joins the ranks of the ancestors. Ayizan stands with the candidate during the second of these births. On the diagram of the

Tree of Life (page 24), the paths or roads of Marie Laveau and Ayizan intersect. Their purities blend and open the door to the most subtle of realms, Atziluth, the archetypal realm that underlies all creation.

Ayizan's aspect in this card is that of a woman walking in the marketplace, her face covered with a palm branch. In this market, both the living and the dead come to vend their wares. The market is a traditional place of power for women. The stock, commodity, money, or fruit markets are but extensions of the life-giving function of a woman's breasts. Until very recently, the newborn baby without a woman to feed it was apt to die. If the market in its various forms were kept and controlled by women, perhaps its function, that of meeting the real needs of the entire populace (female and male) would be fulfilled. It may be a serious aberration that these markets are controlled by men, who use them for personal acquisition and accumulation rather than for life-sustaining functions.

Ayizan's attributes are preservation of the purity of initiation and the bounty of success, pleasure, and happiness provided by the true sight of initiation.

Linda Falorio is a sorceress who has a deep relationship with Ayizan. The presence of Ayizan once came to her as the soul of the Earth. Ayizan was angered by the destruction and fouling of the planet's surface; the loa's rage was deep. Here Ayizan shows another attribute or road she can walk.

CONTEMPLATION

Love as union with the loa through the process of both formal and informal initiation and the purity this entails.

DIVINATION

Love, beauty, pleasure, and success. Protection for women's affairs and the just in general. Concern for purity of devotion.

LOCO
(WILL • THE EMPEROR)

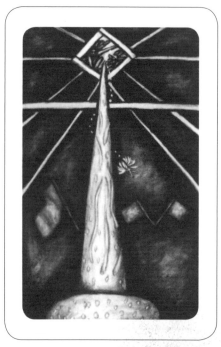

Loco is the racine, or root, loa who walks with Ayizan. He is a guardian of the hounfor and of a variety of the objects it houses. As Ayizan can be described as love, especially in the spiritual sense, Loco can be described as will in the sense of the driving force of magickal acts. If Ayizan is identified as the womb, then Loco is the phallus.

The aspect of Loco depicted in this card shows him looking down through the parted canopy of the forest onto a pole. In the context of the hounfor, or Voodoo Temple, this pole is a central feature and a means through which the loa may enter. A butterfly moving about the card signifies Loco as a guardian of vegetation and one who possesses a profound knowledge of herbs and roots used in curing disease.

His attributes include healing and protection. He is the protector of the center pole and of the whip used in the more militant Petro Voodoo rites. He is a guardian of forests and trees. Compared to Ayizan, the works he performs are more physical, more dense. Loco is said to have called the first dead from the Waters, so he is privy to the mysteries of death.

CONTEMPLATION

The nature of Will. Where the Will finds its origin and upon what ground it gathers power.

DIVINATION

Protection, ambition, victory, strife, conquest, war.

MASTER OF THE HEAD
(SELF • THE HIEROPHANT)

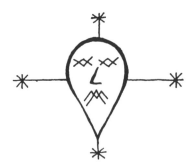

The Master of the Head is the Self on an exalted plain. The Master is the loa that expresses and embodies the highest qualities of an individual. Here the meaning of "master" is not that of an external force controlling an individual, as a term like "schoolmaster" implies. The Master of the Head is the loa capable of integrating the various qualities of the mind and personality into a coherent, directed whole.

This is a great card of initiation. To know and be aligned with the Master of one's Head is to function according to one's own unique place in the universe. One of the most powerful occult axioms is "know yourself," and to know the Master of your Head is to know yourself in a deep and abiding sense.

The aspect of this card is that of a man drumming to bring on full contact with the Master of his Head. As he plays, a face forms on the drum. Mists swirl from the face on the drum's head and become a spirit that kisses the man's upturned forehead.

Attributes of this card include a profound realization of self in an inclusive sense. The union of Love (Ayizan) and Will (Loco), in measure particular to the individual, produces the road upon which the Master of the Head walks.

CONTEMPLATION

True service is always to the Self.

DIVINATION

Realization of purpose, initiation, teachings, assistance from forces perceived as highly placed.

VI

MARASSA
(DUALITY • THE LOVERS OR TWINS)

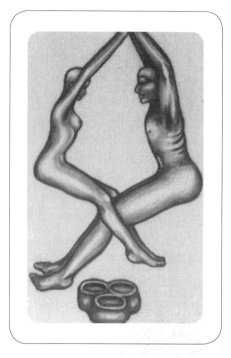

The Marassa are the Divine Twins of the Voodoo pantheon. On the diagram of the Tree of Life they occupy the path of Zain, attributed to the Lovers or Twins (Gemini). The play of these Marassa, or Twins, is that of duality. They are lovers locked in eternal embrace upon the brink of nothingness. Theirs is the existential courage to divide and Be.

The duality which is the Marassa finds its most obvious expression in the symmetry that is one of the shared characteristics of all planetary life forms. The parts that comprise this symmetry are nonantagonistic and dependent upon each other for their very existence.

The position of the figures on the card calls to mind the shape of the vèvè used to call the Marassa. This vèvè is an apt depiction of the axiom, "As above, so below."

The Maràssa are a separate class of being that is quite apart from the loa. They are ancient beyond reckoning. There are many stories that relate the origin of the Twins. Perhaps a Yoruba legend, presented here in a much-shortened form, is most worth telling.

In ancient times there was a man who was a farmer. At his touch the fields sprang to life and the crops were abundant, but the monkeys of the region plagued this farmer. They came again and again, taking much of his produce. In anger, the farmer killed the monkeys who came onto the fields. Still the monkeys persisted.

The farmer's anger grew, and he began to hunt the monkeys in the bush and the forest. Many monkeys were killed, yet the crops continued to be depleted.

The monkeys in their turn grew angry, and two of them entered the womb of the woman who was wife to the farmer. The two monkeys were abukus, or children who die soon after birth. The woman gave birth to twins. Until this time, only monkeys bore twins. This was the first instance of twinned birth among the Yoruba. The twins, being abukus, soon died. They entered the woman time and time again, and each time they died soon after birth.

The woman and the man were desperate and consulted a

diviner. They were told that the twins came from the monkeys. The killing of the monkeys had to cease and the monkeys were to be allowed to eat the crops. They accepted this advice, and the following set of twins lived. The twins had great powers and caused the farm to prosper. Because of their origin the twins are often called edun, meaning monkey.

—**Adapted from Harold Courlander,**
Tales of the Yoruba, Gods and Heroes

This tale of the Twins' origin points out the importance of accepting differences. To actively oppose a force perceived as threatening oftentimes only makes a bad situation worse. Seeking for the means to provide mutual benefit is a powerful way to address potentially disturbing situations.

Their aspect takes the form of a double figure. Male and female touch and take on the form of the Marassa. The three-chambered bowl under the figures is an example of one type of bowl used in services to the Marassa. Two of the chambers are for offerings to the Marassa. The third chamber is an acknowledgment of the fertility of the Marassa; from the two is born all.

The creation and reconciliation of distinctions is their primary attribute.

CONTEMPLATION

The enjoyment of duality as an expression of existence.

DIVINATION

Acceptance of differences. The possibility of turning a perceived threat to your benefit by emphasizing common ground or interests. Childlike qualities; childish fear, anger, or mirth.

VII

DANCE
(MOVEMENT • THE CHARIOT)

The body moves in waves that span the bridge between the visible world of the Living and the world of pure potential. The loa exist in a world of pure movement, where no thing has come into being, no thing has solidified. Now, through the body, through the whirling step of the servitors (those who serve the loa), the loa have found a point of entry. Infinite possibility takes form, and the waves of ecstasy sound a point of creative power.

There is a point at which the dancer leaves and only the dance remains. Sacred dance builds to this point; here a little death occurs and identity is left behind like the skin of a shedding snake. Rider and vehicle become one in movement. Dance is the movement, the vehicle is the dancer, and the rider is the loa.

The aspect depicted in this card is that of the hounsis, initiates who can manifest the loa, dancing in sacred movement. A loa rides the back of one of their number. Here the loa is depicted as a pure being of light, while the hounsi is shown carrying the weight, and thus the possibilities, of matter.

The attributes of this card center on the transcendence of circumstance. A Being of great power is born in the union of hounsi and loa. Spirit bends to embrace matter, and matter returns the favor in kind.

CONTEMPLATION

How little of one's movement the conscious mind directs; even the act of walking is far too complicated for conscious control.

DIVINATION

Transcendence of a situation through ecstatic physical action. Triumph, victory, constructive or destructive adherence to set forms of action.

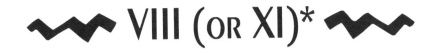

VIII (or XI)*

POSSESSION
(STRENGTH • STRENGTH, LUST)

Dance sets the stage for the drama of possession. Here the question of who dances is answered with style and detail. Lust manifested as divine drunkenness and ecstasy moves the dancer inward to the brink of individual being. The cup runs over, and *self* is obliterated in the torrent of *Self*. Strength, the ability to exert effort toward a given end, is present in the dancer to such a degree that the sacred is drawn within him or her; actions then flow from the sacred's inexhaustible reservoir of grace.

Many fear possession. This is a rational fear, for we are all at risk.

*See table on page 29: Twenty-Two Roads & the Wild Card.

What most of us struggle with is possession by personality. To the extent that we identify with our personalities, we are possessed by that personality's limiting definitions of self. Personality is such an acceptable and pervasive expression of self in society that it is frequently unexamined; it is often mistaken for Self. The boundless wealth of Self comes to be encased in the roles, mores, and expectations of personality. Possession by such a small god strangles the vast array of possibilities inherent in Self.

Quite often what people fear most in ritual possession is a weakening of the hold of the personality on the Self. Personality is a small cage, but it is at least familiar. The greatness of Self can seem foreign, forbidding.

Personality can be of value as a fluid focusing of self in the world. Its structure can be used to create situations and to set the stage for involvements. However, personality is best used, not cast as the user. Ritual possession is one way of breaking free from the confines of a too-deeply entrenched personality.

The aspect of possession portrayed in this card is that of an overwhelming spirit astride the relatively dense body of one of the dancers. The spirit is strong, and this strength is absolutely necessary in order to shape and direct the physical mass of the dancer.

The attributes of possession include willing or voluntary surrender to a force perceived as stronger than the self.

CONTEMPLATION

Who is it that says "I"? What are the aspects and attributes of this "I"? Do they change? Does the "I" change?

DIVINATION

Strength; a bursting free from the bounds of limiting belief; courage and the sufficient energy to act effectively.

COUCHÉ
(INTERNAL INSPIRATION • THE HERMIT)

Couché is the ritual seclusion undergone by prospective initiates before the Mysteries are *revealed* (not answered or explained). This card is one of ritual gestation and birth. Here the candidates partake in the seclusion that precedes birth into another life. The womb's silence and nurturance are invoked to provide an environment for the newfound revelations to grow and flower within the deepest recesses of the candidates. They lie in the fetal position, each cared for by his or her sponsor. A chicken lies at the feet of each candidate, and organic matter anoints their foreheads.

Here it would be good to address the often misunderstood and morbidly emphasized practice of animal sacrifice. We exist in a society that condones the slaughter of vast numbers of animals for food. What is the difference between slaughter and sacrifice? Slaughter is the killing of animals for food, sacrifice the offering of anything to a deity as propitation or homage. The chickens in the card are an example of both slaughter and sacrifice. First they feed the divine within the candidate, and then they are cooked to feed the human. They are a graphic reminder that life feeds on life. If we choose to continue in life, our lives must be worthy of all the lives taken by us that we may continue to move upon this earth.

The aspect of this card is that of a womblike room filled with those who await birth into a new life. They lie in a fetal position on their mats. Life depends on life, so they are sustained by the slaughtered and sacrificed animals at their feet.

The attributes of this card center on sanctuary, the maintenance of a safe space for ritual growth.

CONTEMPLATION

The interdependence of all life. Even our rebirth into a more spiritual plane is dependent upon the lives of what are commonly thought of as lesser beings.

DIVINATION

Retreat from daily life for a spiritual purpose, internal inspiration, realization of the amount others sacrifice that we may grow and prosper; a sense of the sacredness of all life.

THE MARKET
(INTERDEPENDENCE • WHEEL OF FORTUNE)

*All roads lead to the
market.*
—an often-repeated saying

Here the crossroads meet. Movement, change, and flux rule the day. All is interdependence. Gods and mortals barter for that which is necessary to their continued existence. Everything depends upon someone or something else. The loa need the servitors in order to manifest; the servitors need the animals in order to grow physically and spiritually; the animals need the servitors to feed and care for them. If any link in the chain fails, all is lost. If someone takes more than their share, if greed touches the heart of any of the participants, then all must suffer.

This card takes on the aspect of the New Orleans French Market, the oldest operating market in the country. The vendors dressed in purple are a daily sight at the market. They are members of a religious order who come to sell their wares.

The attributes of this card focus on an appreciation of the need for cooperation in order to survive.

CONTEMPLATION

The vast chain of life that supports an individual's existence.

DIVINATION

A realization upon which your works or very existence depends; a rapid change of fortune.

XI (or VIII)*

SECRET SOCIETIES
(BALANCE • JUSTICE, ADJUSTMENT)

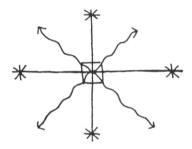

S ecret societies live more in the heart than in the world. Their presence moves through the night of the soul along paths that reach into even the most solitary of places. Iron bars fail at their touch. The night and those who live within it claim the honor and respect due to that which hunts in the deepest tunnels of the soul.

The type of secret society referred to in this card exists more in psychic and psychological dimensions than on a physical plane. There are those who seek to maintain balance in the world through clandestine censure, magick, or force of arms. While their power is great, especially in a land like Haiti, the true power to maintain the balance necessary

*See table on page 29: Twenty-Two Roads & the Wild Card.

for the continuation of life is found within rather than without. When the spirit of community or tradition is violated, something ancient rises to swing the scales back to equilibrium.

This card portrays six wild beasts looking at a kneeling woman. She is in a clearing, and the beasts look on from a swampy jungle. She is dressed in blue and white, colors associated with Agwé and the cleansing power of the sea. Her hands are loosely tied behind her back. On a very deep level, it is her choice to be in the clearing. The ropes do not bind her; their function is more to remind than to restrict. In her hands she holds a guardé, a packet that has been charged with the power of protection by a mambo or houngan. It is the sign of her innocence. The beasts stand and watch. This is the moment before judgment. All is held in a crystalline stillness. The attention of the beasts is aroused, but their attitude is more that of interest than either vengeance or acknowledgment of innocence.

The beasts look on. They bear the aspect of Loup Garou and arise from the deepest levels of human experience. The severest judgment is internal. When the ancestors cry out and lift themselves from the swamp wearing the bodies of powerful beasts, transgression can find no place and the transgressor can find no peace.

Attributes of this card include a righting or balancing of affairs. This restoration of equilibrium takes place on both a very large and a very small scale. Most of the time, this necessary flux is not even noticed; only aberration rises to conscious appreciation.

CONTEMPLATION

Go deeply within, shifting through the shards of broken, ill-formed experience. Move past regret and then past judgment to an appreciation of the part these experiences play in the elegant balance of the universe, both within and without.

DIVINATION

The moment when all hangs in the balance; cases of law, cases of conscience, pangs of conscience calling one to action; recourse to the ancestors for a decision in the matter at hand.

XII

ZOMBI
(SACRIFICE • THE HANGED MAN)

The will has left, purpose has fled. Nothing moves within the head. Nothing moves through stagnant emptiness. Quiet: water drips on rank stone. All is decay: footsteps sound, leading nowhere. Here the Dark will not come and Light will not shine. Here actions know neither success nor failure: conclusion is forgotten in numb repetition. The spider has lost its way on the web: mechanically it moves in circles as the strands vibrate in a thin, dull wind.

There are at least two distinct forms of the Zombi in Voodoo just as there are two forms or types of sacrifice within esoteric tradition. Sacrifice may be enforced or voluntary, its motivation external or internal. The sacrifice of the type of Zombi depicted in this card is enforced, decreed by an external agent (see the discussion of Simbi, page 162, for an alternate form of the Zombi more commonly found in New Orleans).

This is an act of transgression par excellence. The victim helplessly witnesses his or her own death and then continues to live that death. The Zombi may be created by the voodooist as an act of vengeance, for service, or to serve as an example to those who would deeply transgress and strain the bonds of community.

To create is to bring something forth from nothing. With the Zombi, nothing is brought forth from something. Critical in the making of the Zombi is the capture of the victim's Ti Bon Ange (small good angel). The Ti Bon Ange (No. XIV) enables personality to take hold and manifest. When the Ti Bon Ange is captured, the roots of the will are thrust into a slavery that burns like acid.

The aspect of this card is of a woman standing on a slave block within the green mire of a swamp. Her head is thrown back and her arms are thrust up to the heavens in desperation. Just out of reach, the Ti Bon Ange swirls around her hands in the form of a mist. Simbi the snake is wrapped around her waist in promise of possible salvation. The Zombi's mouth has also been sewn shut using a snake as the thread, shutting the Zombi off from the healing power of Naming.

The card's attributes include a form of sacrifice that is externally motivated. To sacrifice is to literally sanctify, to make sacred. What is made sacred by the Zombi? Perhaps it is death and the will itself, which the Zombi sanctifies in perverse reflection. The shape of the Zombi is cast not in light or shadow, it is outcast.

CONTEMPLATION

What rides within the body when the will is lost? What holds the reins?

DIVINATION

Sacrifice externally motivated and enforced. Questions of will and the questioning of will cause resolve to decay and failure of the spirit and/or body.

XIII

LES MORTS
(TRANSFORMATION • DEATH)

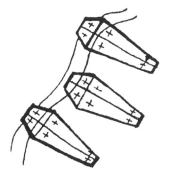

The Morts are the Dead, both named and forgotten. Among their ranks are numbered deceased ancestors. The dead wait in the abyssal waters that ebb and flow beneath the earth. In these waters they wait and watch and, if bidden, reach out with sure fingers to guide and regulate the affairs of the still-living practitioner. They can come again in the bodies of the newborn. The Great Mothers and the Grand Fathers swim in the salty waters of the birth canal, seeking once again the light of the Sun and the Moon. In their coming the covenant that contains all covenants is fulfilled. The new issues from the old in an unbroken spiral of universal flux. The last words of the dying echo in the infant's first cry. The path of the Divine Twins finds holy completion.

—Martinié, 1986

The Les Morts card shows a pair of hands reaching down into the waters to the dead, who swim in a green, swirling cloud pulsing with yellowish power. The hands represent a request for wise counsel and a promise to perform the rites necessary to bring a spirit quickly from the waters. Some of the dead seem to eagerly seek the promise of the hands, while others are content to stare out of the surface of the card or to explore the depths of the waters. A chicken shares their sacred space as a reminder that just as all life is sacred, so all death is also sacred. All beings have their place in the great cycle. Each is of inestimable value.

A primary aspect of this card is motion. All are wrapped in a great swirling tide. Worlds and their beings interpenetrate. Death is not static, and life is not quick. All moves in its own time to its own measure.

CONTEMPLATION

Transformation; a blurring of the boundaries between life and death. Development of the ability to see life in death and death in life.

DIVINATION

Change, flux. Messages from the dead, in particular from the questioner's ancestors. Probable need to make offerings to the ancestors.

XIV

TI BON ANGE
(WILL • ART, TEMPERANCE)

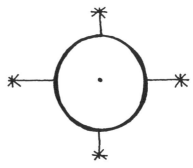

The Ti Bon Ange (small good angel) is clothed in robes of light. The angel stands on a high point and casts a guiding radiance over the dark waters. Ever homeward this light beckons. Remember who you are. Remember the Great Oath taken when nought became two. Turn and return; follow this light into the heart of the Star. There your Name dances upon tongues of flame.

The voice of the Ti Bon Ange has been likened to the conscience. A person's individuality is in many respects defined by the roads or paths he or she chooses. The ability to make this choice emanates from the Ti Bon Ange. This is the core element of the individual, which is trapped and held back when a Zombi is created.

The Ti Bon Ange may be given shelter in a *canari*, clay jar, which is entrusted to the care of a priest or priestess and may be retrieved at any time. This provides a measure of protection from the dangers of malevolent magicks and the vagrancies of chance. This is very similar to the common new-world practice of sorcerers entrusting a talisman containing their essence to a loved one before going on a dangerous etheric expedition. The magickal personality of the sorcerer, if destroyed on the expedition, can be rebuilt from the essence.

The aspect of this card is that of a woman walking from a hut carrying a clay jar upon her head. The Ti Bon Ange is diving into the jar hands first. This jar can be likened to the vessels in the Art or Temperance cards of traditional Tarot. The door of the hut from which the woman walks is open.

Attributes of this card include the exercise and development of will. Will has been described by Aleister Crowley as the factor that points in the direction of the most proper placing of energies, to an individual's unique place in the universe—that place where you are doing what you and you alone can do (1929–30, p. xxii).

CONTEMPLATION

Do what thou wilt, shall be the whole of the Law.

DIVINATION

A call to action based on who you are and your place in the world; assertion of self; discovery of the True Self; an overcoming of obstacles to the expression of the True Self.

XV

COURIR LE MARDI GRAS
(UNCONTROLLED ENERGY • THE DEVIL)

Time stops, caught in the rush of free-fall. Colors circle in drunken reverie. Horses' hooves rise and fall in rhythms that awaken ancient memories. Flung high from the rooftop, a bird touches the stars and then falls down to meet hard, frosted ground. Fate stretches before the eyes in nightmarish landscape. Feathers are splayed in the fierce chill of the wind. Head down, dry mouth open in fear and anticipation. Panic marks the feet and then the hands of the fall. There is no God here but Pan. All else has fled before the hooves and the wind and the sound of flapping wings.

Courir Le Mardi Gras (Run the Mardi Gras) is traditional in southwestern Louisiana. On Fat Tuesday, Cajun men and women dressed in bizarre costumes ride out in the early morning. When farmhouses within the parameters of the Run are approached, their owners climb onto their roofs, each holding a chicken. As the riders circle the house, a chicken is thrown from the rooftop to be fought over by the riders. The winner breaks the chicken's neck and hangs the body from the horse's saddle as a sign to all of the rider's daredevil abilities. The chicken is later used to make gumbo.

The card shows a horned or long-eared figure on the roof of a skull-like hut. A black, red-headed rooster falls through the air toward the Run, which circles the hut. The card conveys an image of wild, unleashed energy quite like the Wild Ride or Wild Hoard of Western mysticism.

Attributes of this card include the material taken to its conclusion, pushed to its limits and beyond. This is the point at which the material turns in upon itself in a burning fury. This is the meaning of Carnival (farewell to flesh). Flesh, or the material, is taken to its extreme and explodes in a brilliant display of sacred frenzy.

CONTEMPLATION

The Self as totally alone yet part of the great web of existence. Star and star, system and system rushing through the universe to courses set by their own individual wills, apart from All yet a part of All.

DIVINATION

Uncontrolled energies; material considerations pushed to their limits; creativity exercised regardless of effect; questions of individuality and interdependence.

XVI

DELUGE
(SACRIFICE • THE BLASTED TOWER)

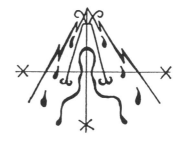

The Waters of the soul are deep and rich. They swirl and leap as if in a calabash stirred by the Ti Bon Ange and the Gros Bon Ange. While all works of the Mind dissolve upon the Waters' coming, the seemingly more tenuous fabrications of Spirit find swift succor in their sweet embrace. These are the Waters of Return. Everything is ever as it was, nothing is changed. The touch of the Waters declares this truth. Their swift fingers chip at the Mind and its beliefs. Thoughts fall and are carried back to their source. The Land below the Waters, the Land of the Spirits, calls out and gathers in. From the Waters we came, and to the Waters we will return.

The Ti Bon Ange (will) and the Gros Bon Ange (love) join together and create within themselves the emptiness of self. The sacred calabash, or gourd, is empty. Nothing moves within its walls. To create is to bring something forth from nothing. This is the Work of the Angels. The self of the voodooist is like the sacred calabash. It is empty, open to the act of creation, open to the touch of the Angels. This self has been washed clean by the Waters. The Mind and its beliefs, whether true or false, can embrace only a small part of existence. The Waters flow within and through All.

The Self is like a child covered with the dust of play. The Waters come to wash, refresh, and empty its essential being. Wisdom is what is left (conversation with Mishlen Linden, 1991). The Waters are the guardian of wisdom.

This card depicts lightning striking an electrical tower and the Mississippi River. The force of the storm drives the river over the levee. The levee breaks and a car, house, and road are swept away. The Waters reach out to recover the land taken from them. The blue sky reflects the blue waters. . . . As above, so below. The images of this card are taken from an area of New Orleans known as Riverbend. The land between the levee and the river is a popular site for ritual. Pieces of colorful cloth hang from the trees, and on the ground are numerous places of worship and sacrifice. When contemplating the Waters, it is always good to remember that much of the city of New Orleans is below sea level.

Attributes of the card include inevitable sacrifice. Sacrifice and sacred are derived from the same root: To (sacr)ifice is to make (sacr)ed. The Waters will come sooner or later, whether bidden or unbidden. The dust will be washed away to reveal the empty core. This card contains the key to immortality. If we identify with the dust, we will be carried back to the source. If we identify with the empty core, the hollowness of the calabash, there will be nothing for the Waters to touch, and from this emptiness our voices will be as those of the loa.

CONTEMPLATION

To resist the Waters is to cling to dust.

DIVINATION

Sacrifice, unavoidable and often misunderstood; violent physical or emotional upheaval revealing core issues or aspects of the self.

XVII

Z'ÉTOILE
(A CLEAR ROAD • THE STAR)

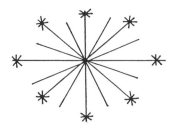

In the day there is but one light; in the night there are many. Every man and every woman is a star (Crowley, 1938). Fate upon fate, destiny upon destiny revolve across the Heavens as distant pinpoints of light. Night's abyss serves as the womb of magickal birth. As above, so below . . . Every man and every woman is a star.

In the day our sun provides equal light to all; the night is the time of subtle influences. Our star holds our destiny. Here the reference is not so much to the physical entity that roams the distant skies, but to the interplay between the light cast by a particular star and the light emitted by a zone of power situated at the top of the head (called in the east the Crown Chakra). The link between the light of the Star and the light that emanates from the top of the head appears as a tube or tunnel, which allows direct communication with the reservoir of our destiny (conversation with Mishlen Linden, 1989).

The star can be visualized as a calabash, or large hollow gourd, containing our destiny. The great African oracle Ifa is composed of descriptive readings known as *odu*, which can be understood as "big calabash" (Gleason, 1973, p. 11). In this sense, Ifa presents our destiny as contained within the calabash. It is as if these *odu* in the form of stars trace the brilliant lines of destiny across the face of the night sky.

The "dark night of the soul" occurs when sight of the Star and sense of connection with the Star is lost. Then the practitioner is seemingly cut off from his or her destiny. The road is blocked. Efforts to break through end in failure or drag on into repetition, devoid of result. If Z'Étoile is positioned in a reading to cross the questioner, this dark night can be expected. Experience teaches that the dark night is most likely to yield benefit if it is viewed as a form of communication between the universe and the self. Look where the blockages lie; see if they leave a trail leading back to actions or lack of action that offended the loa or ancestors. Perhaps sacrifice is called for, perhaps a change of action.

The aspect of the card is that of a babe in an egg, sucking his or her thumb as the egg floats in the black of outer space, or the womb. Streamers of light swirl around the egg and careen into the darkness. These streamers are the basis of the connection between the head and the star.

Attributes of the card include the search for an understanding of one's destiny. Doubts drop away and the road is clear.

CONTEMPLATION

Look into the night sky, star upon star, system upon system. Feel for the star that carries your fate.

DIVINATION

Coming to terms with one's fate and obtaining the clear sight and strength this action brings, dedication to a lifework. The road is clear, the Star in sight.

XVIII

MAGICK MIRROR
(MAGICK • THE MOON)

Here there is danger; here the line dividing the worlds grows thin. Here the crust upon which we walk grows tenuous in the mists. The worlds meet and join hands, right to left, left to right. The Waters have risen above the heavens and fallen below the earth . . . now they rest in an illusion of solidity. The mirror is these Waters frozen in time. Deception and true sight play upon its surface, and the loa reach out from its depths. The mirror is the magickal weapon par excellence, equally able to trap the user or that which is summoned within its watery realm. This is the card of magick and sorcery.

The magicks of the mirror are strong and ancient. Upon the surface of the mirror the worlds meet. The world of the Great Invisibles and the visible material world mirror one another. It is as if the Waters flow in opposite directions on either side of the Mirror. The surface of the mirror is the point where the two opposite streams meet. The tension of their contact creates the illusion of solidity, but the stability of the surface is easily broken by the touch of the sorcerer's will. Once its equilibrium is disturbed, the Waters surge forth or push inward with tremendous force. They can be used to carry an expedition through the protections of another sorcerer but if control is lost, their force can turn and carry the same malevolent powers into the spellworker's heart.

It is common for voodooists to mirror one other's actions in the performance of the rites. This can have different significance in different contexts. When ritualistic gestures of greeting and recognition are exchanged, the mirroring may constitute a show of unity. It may also be used in a contest of strength in which two powerful practitioners compete through a performance of mirrored, complex, ritual gestures. A strong magickal charge is built up and exchanged through the performance of these gestures, and the concentration of one of the participants usually vacillates and breaks. While the above two contexts for the mirroring of gestures are fairly straightforward, the third context is more pervasive and more obscure. In this case the mirroring serves to acknowledge and ritualistically invoke the doubled nature of visible existence and the invisible spirits so aptly displayed by the twins, the Marassa. This doubling is a great mystery; to experience its essence is to have the underpinnings of one's "reality" shorn through.

The aspect of this card is that of a mirror surrounded by stars. The mirror rises from the blue Waters against a background of purple space. A birdlike lunar figure hovers in the upper right-hand corner of the card. The bird is identified with sorcery in the African oracle Ifa: "Work of hands, wings shall despoil—such be our intentions" (Gleason, 1973, p. 133).

A primary attribute of this card is symmetry. Like meets like in opposite stance upon the mirror's surface. This relates the Mirror directly to the Marassa (No. VI). The Divine Twins are duality, and duality is the domain of magick.

CONTEMPLATION

Look into the mirror until your image moves while you are still. Here magick begins.

DIVINATION

Magick and sorcery, occult power, deception.

XIX

GROS BON ANGE
(LOVE • THE SUN)

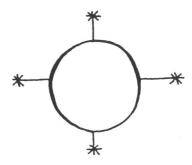

Honor and respect to the night. Outside the city's bright veil, all sleep secure in bed and house. The roads are empty and clear, save for those who walk in darkness. First light breaks, and all begin to stir.

Praise to You whose rays warm the Marassa in their play.
Praise to You whose touch is sweet to Twins.
Praise to You twice blessed with fire and fury.

Praise to You Grand Road of old Legba.
Praise to You upon whose point Legba walks.
Praise to You whose light streams through open door.

Praise to You who shone upon our ancestors.

Praise to You by whose light our ancestors walked.
Praise to You in whose light all dead once walked.

Praise to You in cloak of forty colors.
Praise to You in whose fires the sacred names of Spirits dance.
Praise to You bright eye of the sky loa.

Praise to You whose fires warm the Waters.
Praise to You who walk in brilliance.
Praise to You born of the womb of night.
Praise to You of grace freely given.
Praise to You brightness of the Orient.

You are the tongues of flame which speak the Spirit's most Holy Name.
You who unite all in common chorus, Your praise names we sing.
In this and evermore, your tidings we bring.

Outside the city with its entertainment and constant diversion, darkness holds the land. Solitude—what business has someone under a neighbor's window or in a neighbor's yard? The dark of night is a time of privacy, of individual prerogative. This is the time of magick. This is the time when the secret societies take to the streets. With the coming of light, the phantasmagoria of the night settles into more regular patterns. Day is a time of community. The individual will joins in action with that of the group.

As Z'Étoile is destiny and the Ti Bon Ange is will, so the Gros Bon Ange is love. This love (union) is the stuff of existence. As the Sun shines on both good and bad, so this love is unconditional; it wraps and holds all things. Equally beneficent is this love; it gives its all to each without thought of time or place, right or wrong. As such it is not dependent upon personal traits. The Gros Bon Ange carries the grace of the spirit. The Ti Bon Ange holds within itself the ability to choose to employ this grace. Love is the road that Will walks, guided by the Star.

The aspect of this card is one of dynamic movement. The sun is depicted against a purple background. Yellow rays containing small figures swirl out from the central orb.

A primary attribute of this card is energy. The sun provides the energy necessary for physical life on our planet through the process of fission, the breaking apart of atoms. The Gros Bon Ange supplies the energy for the spiritual life of the individual through the power of love or the uniting of dualities (Marassa, the Twins). Here again, as in a mirror, the processes of the Invisible World reflect those of the Visible World in reverse fashion.

CONTEMPLATION

Love is the road that Will walks, guided by the Star.

DIVINATION

Influx of helpful energy; success possibly earned by effort or possibly not. Love freely given without regard to object; happiness, joy. Universal rather than particular love.

XX

ANCESTORS
(RESPECT • AEON, LAST JUDGMENT)

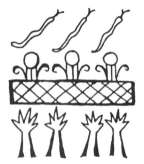

The voices of thousands of souls cry out within us. The hands of the ancestors weave our destiny with threads whose beginnings are dipped into the waters of creation. To hear the cry of these souls, to feel the twistings of this thread, is to know our Name in its most pregnant fullness. We are heir to a largeness that knows no end and is touched by no beginning.

The ancestors speak words of wisdom: Be strong. Be sensitive. Touch life fully. Drink deeply. Our Names walk within your head. We taste with your lips. We walk with your feet. All that you are, we were. All that you will be, we will become. We stand spread against the great globe of the sky. Face upon face, Name upon Name, we inform your actions. Deep within the land under the Waters, our feet walk your road. We are the cup that measures your largeness.

Vast or small is our number . . . choose well. In honoring us, you honor yourself. In praising our Names, you praise your own Name.

The ancestors are those dead whom we take as having directly influenced our becoming. The number of ancestors we acknowledge can be great or small. Family, tribe, nation, people, all these can be counted as ancestors. There is no correct choice. The ancestors will speak to you their Names; their voices are life and its happenings. There is great benefit in honoring one's ancestors, just as there is great danger in ignoring their voices.

The aspect of this card is that of a float ridden by the loa. They throw gold and beads that turn to snakes as they fall into the waiting hands of the crowd. This is an allusion to the snake vertebra used to create necklaces of power and significance. The float itself has a green snake painted on its side. This is Simbi, the patron of magick. The presence of the loa in the depiction of this card emphasizes that many of these great spirits once lived and walked the earth as women and men. They can be claimed as ancestor.

The forms taken by the loa are those of Egyptian deities. The lore of the Tarot holds Egypt as its ancestor or point of origin. Horus of the hawk's head throws beads while making the Western mystical sign for the rending and closing of the veil. Hoor-paar-kraat, with his finger to his lips, gives the sign of silence. This card shows a diversity of ancestral influences come together to create a tableau vivant, or living picture, of Voodoo's accepting, inclusive nature.

A primary attribute of this card is respect. When a voodooist respects the ancestors, she or he respects her- or himself. Respect literally means "to look at": what is seen in the ancestors are aspects and attributes the self may develop in this life.

CONTEMPLATION

Remember the names of as many ancestors as you can; let your mind open to the fullness of these names. If other names present themselves, respect these also as ancestors.

DIVINATION

Final judgment, an understanding of the worth and meaning of one's actions within the context of the procession of life.

XXI

CARNIVAL
(RELEASE • THE WORLD, THE UNIVERSE)

The flames of desire rise. Into that furnace all longings are fed. Revelry stokes the fires to white-hot brightness. Come now, hold back not a whim. All is expended. In drunken sleepless pleasures, longing is sated. This is the World. Drink deeply. Take your will and fill of love. The soul delights in the body's fulfillment. The spirit turns outward through the body's senses. To they who hold back nothing, nothing will be withheld. To they who give all, all will be given. The Courir of the country is matched by the more refined parades of the city. The chicken is replaced with beads and pentacles. The city's hands reach not for food, but for adornment. With the flesh one turns outward to taste, touch, feel, smell—all senses are enraptured in the celebration of the World and its offerings.

In Carnival the World erupts in cascading delight. Bodies give themselves to the revel and in so doing open their spirits to the sweet touch of revelation. Masked faces twist in the abandonment of self. Behind the great mask of Carnival, the small masks worn in the everyday world disappear. Sacred time touches all action, as clocks round their regular twelve, twelve, twelve with unnoticed precision. The Carnival, the Revel is ever Now.

The revel is a time of revelation and also of a revolving. Now the Wheel of Tarot turns back upon itself. The strands of beads thrown from the floats and worn during Mardi Gras become the snakes hatched from the World Egg (No. 0). The cycle is complete. An end is always a beginning, and beginning is but another word for end.

The Carnivals of Rio, New Orleans, and Venice tie these cities together in a sisterhood of spirit. Carnival, literally a "farewell to flesh," describes a period of turning outward that precedes a time of inward movement. The dynamic flux of equilibrium is upheld.

There is a note of danger in Carnival. The masks of the revel can be used by one's enemies to act without detection. There are those who leave New Orleans during Mardi Gras to escape possible retribution for wrongs committed during the year. Anyone might approach in the masked crowds, strike, and then disappear, one mask among many.

The aspect of this card is a night lit by masked flambeau (naphtha torch) carriers. Three lights are held aloft; three is the number of Legba, the loa who opens the door between the worlds. The flambeau also brings to mind the Hebrew letter *shin*, a glyph attributed to spirit. Snakes, instead of beads, rain upon the crowd. A woman with a beaded headdress stands at the front of the float. Her face is covered. She is the maiden aspect of Erzulie, clothed in mystery. She is ever the virgin in that the World and its experiences are ever new to her.

A primary attribute of Carnival is release. This release is definitely not from the World. The World, together with all the marvelous experiences it offers, is a part of this liberation. The release is from smallness to more complete awareness of our ways and states of being. This would include a consciousness of the factors that we control and those factors that act through us.

There is no growth; we are ever complete. What increases is awareness, the ability to focus one's attention and to appreciate that in the final, formal elegance of *maya* (illusion) the beauty of spirit is revealed.

CONTEMPLATION

Carnival . . . Farewell to flesh.

DIVINATION

Points to a greater appreciation of the elements of the question or concern that is addressed in the reading. Physical aspects of the question or concern; release from a problem through physical means.

~~ WILD CARD ~~

THE BARONS
(THE BARONS • UNEXPECTED CHANGE)

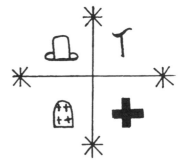

Papa Gèdé bel ga'çon!
Papa Gèdé bel ga'çon!
L'habillé tout ennoi'!
Pou'l monté au palais!

Papa Gèdé is a handsome fellow!
Papa Gèdé is a handsome fellow!
He is dressed all in black
For he is going to the palace!

—quoted by Harold Courlander,
The Drum and the Hoe, p. 58.

T he Barons belong to and lead the family of Guedeh spirits. These Guedeh Barons are not spirits of the dead, but the spirit of Death itself.

It seems that many years ago, under the régime of President Borno [1922–1930], there suddenly appeared in the streets of Port-au-Prince a crowd of Ghedes . . . wearing the formal costume . . . the tall top hats, long black coat-tails, smoked glasses, cigarettes or cigars, and canes. An enormous crowd naturally collected around them, and joined them in their march to the National Palace. They all took the guards by surprise, and, singing, swerved through the gates and up the drive and to the door itself, where they demanded money of the President. President Borno, who is reputed to have been sympathetic to Voudoun ritual (secretly so) and yet feared bourgeois opinion, was in a great dilemma. He finally gave in . . . and the Ghedes with their supporters left the grounds.

—Maya Deren, *Divine Horsemen*, p. 107

The personalities of the Barons are a mixture of irreverent humor, sex, and death. Their presence is not so much frightening as unsettling. They are highly cultured, the ultimate urbane sophisticate of the Voodoo pantheon. It is traditional that the first male buried in a cemetery be regarded as the Baron and that the first female be regarded as Manman Brigitte, a powerful loa, judge, and lawyer of high regard. The Baron and Manman Brigitte are seen as married.

The connections that can be drawn between sex and death are numerous. Sexual reproduction necessitates death; the orgasm itself is often called "the little death." An organism that reproduces itself asexually by splitting or fission avoids death; it is, barring disaster, immortal. In a sense it has traded individuality for immortality. The Barons, on the other hand, are extreme in their expression of individuality. They are apt to take (who can say that a spirit steals?) food from other loa and disrupt otherwise orderly ceremonies. The Barons' sexuality is ribald and lewd, poking fun at the means of life's continuation and death's reason for being.

The Barons are numerous, but three of their number are most often honored. These are Baron Samedi, Baron La Croix, and Baron Cimetière. Their aspect is not that of the somber Horsemen of the Apocalypse; they are horsemen of a different type. They are often gay, delighting in the pleasures of life. They do not come in judgment, bringing scourge and plague. The horses they ride are not the lean creatures of the Apocalypse but are well-fed and pampered.

The aspect of this card is that of the Barons and Manman Brigitte climbing the steps of the French Quarter Police Station as part of projected Day of the Dead celebrations in New Orleans. The police, city hall, and the Haitian palace represent a sense of order or security maintained from without. Death, in its aspect as clown, easily pierces all such vanities. No walls, however thick or rich or well protected, can stop or even slow its progress.

CONTEMPLATION

Death as the great equalizer, pricking vanities both large and small.

DIVINATION

Extreme unexpected turn of events; a sense of humor pulls one through dire circumstances.

FORTY
SPIRITS

THE FOUR ACES

KETHER

UNDERLYING OR ROOT POWERS; THE CREATOR

The four aces are attributed to Kether, the first vessel of the Tree of Life; they depict the most pure influence of fire, water, air, and earth. Here energy is in its most pure state, and therefore the symbolism of the snake is used for three of the four cards. The royal serpent is an apt depiction of pure consciousness focused in a state of un-adulterated attention. The quiet concentration of the serpent reminds us of the deepest states of contemplation. The contemplation following the card's description is meant to assist the practitioner in entering this state. Some voodooists believe that the human soul passes into the body of a serpent after lifetimes of purification; perhaps the act of contemplation gives a small taste of the serpent's powers.

It would be worthwhile to mention here the association of the serpent with evil in the Roman Catholic religion. Great religious truths are expressed through symbols. These truths may (or may not) be applicable to all people across all cultures, but the symbols in which they are conveyed are more times than not tied to a particular time and a particular place. The Roman religion found its origin in the desert people of the Old Testament. The serpents that inhabit deserts are apt to be of more querulous disposition than are serpents in general. For a desert people to represent evil as a serpent is understandable. Peoples of the temperate or tropical zones are more likely to come across peaceful snakes; therefore, when the serpent is used as a symbol by people of these zones, it is not as apt to be depicted as evil incarnate.

PETRO • FIRE
DAMBALLAH
LA FLAMBEAU

In this card, Damballah blazes with the fires of life. Damballah's eyes and body are red to show that in this manifestation he is all fire and force, pure active energy. Here the fire-breathing serpent begins to meld with the attributes of the Dragon.

The primary attribute of this card is the vigor of fire.

CONTEMPLATION

Damballah climbing the center pole of the Voodoo Temple, an outward sign or manifestation of the Kundalini of the East rising up the spine.

DIVINATION

Natural force, strength, and energy are available for use. If the reading indicates opposition by this card, the questioner may expect to meet with strong antagonism.

CONGO • WATER
AYIDA WEDO

Ayida Wedo is the rainbow, the Feathered Sky Serpent. The rainbow is the bridge between the heavens and the earth; a road the Great Invisibles may walk. Here water is the creative force.

The card depicts a snake dancer who through the dance has joined with the serpent in such a deep manner that one is almost indistinguishable from the other. The dancer has formed an ecstatic union with the snake.

The ability to exert pressure is an attribute of the serpent. This constricting force can be used as a means of contact or communication. It allows for a profound physical, psychological, and spiritual joining (conversation with Muslima Moonpaki, 1990). This pressure (not to the neck) is a key to the use of snakes in certain Voodoo trances.

CONTEMPLATION

Pressure. In one of their manifestations, the Waters are the astral menstruum. This unseen element flows around the body, exerting pressure on it. Trace the pressures that exert themselves on the body.

Move from the most apparent to the most subtle. What information, what messages do these touches or pressures bring?

DIVINATION

This card points to pleasure and happiness. The influence is that of the Great Mother, who creates freely through the subtle pressure of the Waters.

RADA • AIR
DAMBALLAH
WEDO

Damballah is the Great Serpent. "Da" as a root refers to the serpent or the serpent's power. Damballah stretches as a link between the voodooist and the wisdom and power of the ancestors. On his back and the back of Ayida Wedo are carried all unnamed ancestors, those ancestors whose names have been lost in the seas of time.

In this card, Damballah Wedo hangs in the air from a crossroads created by the branches of the Sacred Tree. He hangs serenely, in perfect balance. There is no tendency toward movement in any direction. The force of this card can move in a helpful or a hurtful direction, but only after it is called. If left to its own devices, the serpent will continue to hang in its perfect, airy perch.

The primary attribute of this card is attention pressed into action. The eggs that fall from Damballah's perch represent the potential for this action.

CONTEMPLATION
Move into a space of perfect stillness. See from behind your eyes.

Locate yourself deep within your body. Will a specific movement, such as a slight lifting of the fingers. Trace the impulse as it travels from stillness to action.

DIVINATION

Great energy called to do good or ill. Stationary forces are roused and called into action.

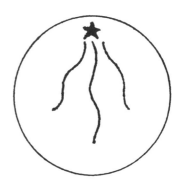

SANTERÍA • EARTH
OLODUMARE

Olodumare, the Creator in the religion of Santería, is depicted in this card. Olodumare is composed of three distinct spirits, and these three spirits are shown descending upon the Earth to create Obatalá, a patron of peace and purity. This act of creation is pictured using a tearlike image. Sorrow plays a part in this card. The initial human whose creation was sanctioned by Olodumare turned against the Creator due to pride. What we are witnessing in this card is the second act of creation, tinged with the sorrow engendered by the first failure.

Attributes of this card include solidification of will and being prone to the sorrow that at some time touches all creators and parents.

CONTEMPLATION
Accepting one's personal failures. Embracing one's sadness. Using these sadnesses and failures to build a house of peace and purity, an impregnable abode fit for the indwelling of Obatalá.

DIVINATION

The root sense of materiality. The presence of all material possibilities, from soaring wealth to crushing poverty.

THE FOUR TWOS
CHOKMAH

PROJECTION, MOVEMENT, CHANGE

Chokmah is the second vessel of the Tree of Life and provides the matrix for the forces projected by the four twos. It is in Chokmah that the attentiveness of the snake, attributed to Kether, is translated into movement. The line, a symbol of Chokmah, is also an apt glyph of the serpent. It is interesting to note that the letter *yod*, which is likewise attributed to Chokmah, has a form that displays a snakelike undulation. The similarity between snake and sperm, a corrolate of Chokmah, is also visually apparent. The Serpent's movement and thus exploration imparts knowledge, the key word of Chokmah.

Nan Nan Bouclou is feminine, although Chokmah is generally conceived to be a "male" vessel. This confusion or contradiction is understandable within the context of the lore of the Kabala. Kabalistic lore holds that there is a great chasm or abyss between the first three vessels and their seven companions. This abyss is similar to the surface of a mirror; that which passes through is reversed. The reversal of gender pays homage to the power of this kabalistic "mirror." Binah, the third vessel, follows suit by predominantly using a male loa to depict the virtues of a "female" vessel.

PETRO • FIRE
NAN NAN
BOUCLOU
LA FLAMBEAU

With this card, the power of Nan Nan Bouclou is expressed through the medium of spiritual fire. Her spiritual initiations bestow individual awareness and knowledge. Her staff has become a hollow tube used to transmit the fires of initiation, the fires of knowledge. In this sense it is similar to the flame of the Christian Pentecost. Nan Nan Bouclou La Flambeau is a loa of spiritual fire. As represented in this card, she is the force that ensures the continuance of both the universe and the individual. Her fire burns in star and hearth. Born of nothing and dependent upon nothing for its continued existence, this fire is the basis of harmonious individuality. It is will in pure form.

This card shows a female loa blowing fire through a hollow tube. The spiritual fire is transmitted outward. In this card, Nan Nan Bouclou La Flambeau is identified with the fire itself, as in the card of Air she is identified with the forest and the herbs themselves. The spiritual fire pierces the foreheads of those persons nearby, imparting a primary infusion of will.

At one and the same time, these sparks are both the basis of individual will and the links connecting individual will to the ebb and flow of the universe. This is a depiction of the creation of individual will and of individuality itself.

CONTEMPLATION
Will as the basis of both individual action and cooperation.

DIVINATION
Influence; individual will focused in such a way as to bring change upon another, for good or ill.

CONGO • WATER
GRAN IBO

Gran Ibo is the old wise woman of the swamp. Within her the secrets of the swamp revolve in a rhythm characterized by age and patience. This loa concentrates or focuses the powers of water. She lives within the mysteries of the swamp, and through her the roots, plants, and flowers of the swamp speak to the voodooist. As with Nan Nan Bouclou, there is a strong emphasis on healing. Gran Ibo is a contact or link between the world of the voodooist and something vast and ancient. She is a loa who embodies experience ancient beyond memory. Old beyond time, she walks among the root loa. Gran Ibo is the heart of the forest. She and the forest are one in their being.

The aspect of this card is that of an elder sitting on a porch, looking into the heart of the swamp. She sits and she waits and she watches. From her close watching grows wisdom. The mysteries of the swamp come to her. They are drawn out by the intensity and focus of her attention. A yellow canary, one of her sacred animals, whispers secrets into her ear. She hears and understands the languages of all the life forms that surround her. Her presence radiates a wisdom most often associated with first or primary things.

CONTEMPLATION

Go into a swamp or wet place. Observe and listen to life in its myriad manifestations. Seek the one voice behind all the sights and sounds.

DIVINATION

Harmony born of a deep and abiding wisdom. A marriage in the Visible or Invisible World as an expression of harmony, plenty.

RADA • AIR
NAN NAN
BOUCLOU

Nan Nan Bouclou is the Grand Mother. From her came the Twins, and to the Twins all that exists can trace its ancestry. The deuces of Chokmah are her issue. Crowley spoke of creation in terms of the equation $0 = 2$. Zero is the cipher of origin; this zero can be seen as the womb of Nan Nan Bouclou, from which the two, or the sacred Twins (Marassa), sprang. This Grand Mother, who existed even before the Twins, is a loa of herbs and medicines. Medicine is a very special type of food; with the medicines of Nan Nan Bouclou, there is a movement beyond the purely physical act of eating to a type of ingestion that transcends hunger and moves toward concern. Medicines as gifts of the earth are her special province. In Western occultism the element of air is associated with the mind, and the purest, most beneficial use of the mind is formed in the study of medicines and healing powders.

Variations in the spelling of her name include Nananbouclou, Nanan Bouloucou, and Nana Bukuu. She is an ancient root loa who has many faces and can take many forms. The original African deity Nana Bukuu is of great importance. "The name of Nana is famous from Ife in Nigeria to Siade and Tchari in Ghana. . . . She herself was a superlative warrior, utterly fearless, who razed the mythic city of Teju-ade" (Thompson, 1983, p. 68).

Within the context of these cards and Voodoo practice, her aspects as creator and healer are emphasized. But her African origins as warrior serve well her position in Chokmah in that, upon crossing the mirror or abyss, the power of Chokmah feeds into the warlike vessel of Geburah.

The card shows two men gathering roots and herbs under a tree. Nan Nan Bouclou is present as the forest itself, which provides medicines and ingredients for powders. One man holds a root that looks like a mandrake. Mandrake is an important element in a number of Western magickal spells. The mandrake root is said to take the shape of a miniature man or woman, and to find one of these roots is to gain access to great power. The men depicted in the card freely share their knowledge, openly showing their findings to one another.

CONTEMPLATION

Creation through the principle of 0 = 2. The zero as the womb of Nan Nan Bouclou and the two as the Marassa.

DIVINATION

Mutual benefit based upon the experience of and devotion to the Grand Mother.

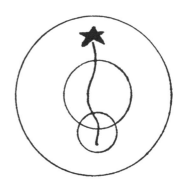

SANTERÍA • EARTH
OLOFI

Silence hangs like a veil. Within this silence, a trinity of orisha move. They are the first. They wield the power of aché, the lifeblood of the universe. Nzalam, Baba Nkwa, and Olofi move within the unspeakable greatness of Olodumare, the unknowable source of all being.

Olodumare brings forth life on the Earth. The new life fails due to pride; the planet is wiped clean and once again the beginnings of life are introduced. Two Spirits of the great Olodumare, Nzalam and Baba Nkwa, leave to continue their work elsewhere. The orisha Olofi remains. Olofi is the personal deity of this planet. The aché that flows through this orisha's veins also flows through every moving, living, or creative element of Earth.

This card shows a pregnant woman suspended in space. The Earth forms and swells within her belly. Spirits swirl around her and the planets seem to have gathered to watch and pay respect to the act of her giving birth. The orisha Olofi, so strongly connected to creation, is represented by this Star Mother.

One attribute of aché shows itself in the world as change. Stability is a process of change; any sense or perception of stability is found upon examination to be the result of an ongoing flux. This flux is necessary to maintain the dynamic balance of elements we perceive as stability or solidity.

CONTEMPLATION

Aché manifesting as change and change as stability.

DIVINATION

Change, especially that change that brings stability to a situation or relationship.

THE FOUR THREES

BINAH

SEX, DEATH

Morning Libations

The first liquids of the day are offered to the dead.

Before refreshing yourself, fill a cup with coffee, water, or some other liquid and stand over an open piece of ground.

Holding the cup with both hands, inscribe a crossroads in the air in front of you. Pass the liquid through the center of the crossroads with a slight throwing motion. Allow the cup to leave the grasp of your hand for a split second as it passes through the crossroads. Say, "To all who have come before."

"To those who are named." (Here repeat the names of those dead you wish to remember.) Pour out a bit of the liquid.

"To those whose names have been forgotten, lost in the seas of Time." Pour out a bit of liquid.

"To those whose bones lie within and upon this land." Pour out a bit of liquid.

Raise the cup up with both hands. "To you from the living."

Take the first drink of the day.

Binah is the third vessel on the Tree of Life. Binah and Chokmah, corresponding to Guedeh and Nan Nan Bouclou, are the great Marassa, or Twins, who sit in the topmost branches of the Tree of Life. They are birthed from the egg of Ayida Wedo and Damballah Wedo (Kether). Kether is that fathomless point into which the grace or aché of God—Bon Dieu Bon of Voodoo or Olodumare of Santería—is channeled.

Binah is love to Chokmah's will. Joined together in the manner of Marassa, they birth the so-called false vessel, Daath, the abode of the Barons (the Wild Card or Joker of this deck). Through the Barons, the grace of Bon Dieu Bon winds its way to the World or Malkuth, the tenth vessel. In a very real sense the Barons own the world, as their title "baron" (landholder; an ancient term encompassing all nobility) implies. The Barons lead the dead, and it is the bodies of the dead upon which we walk in our daily business. Since the dawning of life, all who have come before us lie within the earth. The land on which we walk rebuilds and renews itself, using the bodies of the dead. This is the last step of the food chain. Our bodies eat of the earth and then are eaten by the earth.

Binah is home to the family of Guedeh spirits, those loa who hold safe the forgotten dead who otherwise would be nameless and unhonored. It is through Guedeh that these dead are praised. Their names revolve within him safe from the strong winds of oblivion.

The love of the Guedehs is expressed through the twin forces of sex and death. Sex promises the voodooist continuation in the Visible World. Death holds the promise of continuation in the Invisible World. Through the grace of sex, souls are born into this world. Through the grace of death, ancestors are born into the world of the Invisibles. The womb and the tomb walk hand in hand in the sphere of the Guedehs. They are both places of passage, of initiation.

The Guedehs and the Barons are very close in style and definition. In this deck, the Guedehs are associated with the unnamed dead in the Morning Libation, and the Barons are associated with the known dead. The Barons lead, or more properly, walk before the Guedehs.

This is more an expression of temporal proximity to the living voodooist than of hierarchical positioning.

The primary attribute and title of this vessel is Understanding. This title is very literal: to understand is to literally "stand under." Understanding is the product of "standing under" that which is to be understood and opening one's self up. In times of poetry and magick one can, for example, "under stand" the night sky.

Binah is home to the Great Sea, which promises birth and continuation. The shell of this vessel also contains the City of the Pyramids, that vast necropolis wherein adepts working the Tree of Life sit and wait and experience a thorough cleansing and elevation. The womb-tomb is the form through which sex and death are expressed.

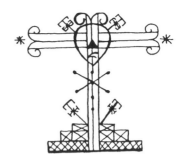

PETRO • FIRE
GUEDEH
LA FLAMBEAU

In Guedeh La Flambeau burns the fire of Binah. This loa shines brightly in the darkness of the womb-tomb. His soul bursts with a radiance not unlike that of Lucifer, bright angel of the morning. If Guedeh is a bright ember burning through the darkness of the grave, then Guedeh La Flambeau is the flashing brilliance of the orgasm, often called "the little death." This Guedeh is the instant of brilliant seduction experienced by the moth before its body joins with the flame it loves so much.

The aspect of this card is that of a strongly sexual male Guedeh embracing a woman. His hand is between his legs to further enflame himself. The woman, literally swept off her feet, holds tightly to the Guedeh's neck.

The primary attribute of this card is force and strength, particularly of a sexual nature.

CONTEMPLATION

Sexual excitement appears as a roaring furnace. This furnace burns in the tomblike basement of a cold, old building. Approach the furnace and bask in its heat.

DIVINATION

Power, strength, magnetism, all generally—though not necessarily—of a sexual nature. Possible tendency toward arrogance.

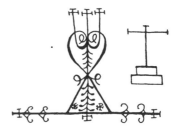

CONGO • WATER MANMAN BRIGITTE

Manman Brigitte's card is water within the realm of Binah. Manman Brigitte calls Guedeh her husband and rules, along with him, the grounds of the cemetery. She is renowned as a judge and lawyer. She is one of the highest powers before whom the voodooist can plead his or her case. In the role of judge and lawyer she is just, for she has balanced the great forces of Binah. In her, life and death embrace and gently rock back and forth to the measured beat of the court drum.

Manman Brigitte is change; she is closely associated with Kali. She is fearsome only if change is resisted. Those close to her realize that the price of stability is change. It is the love and devotion of her servitors that give her life, that allow her to walk in the world of the living. It is their "under standing" that brings Brigitte into the beauty of the World.

Her aspect in this card is that of a corpselike woman sitting on a pile of stones. This pile of stones is her altar and is often erected to her in cemeteries. The tree in this card is an elm, and the lit candles are placed before her by her servitors. Seated atop her stone altar, she is reminiscent of those adepts who in their meditative positions comprise the City of Pyramids.

Her primary attribute is wise judgment. Falsehood withers at her touch. No lies can abide in the solemn depth of her quiet. If proper judgment is exercised on the part of the voodooist, if death and life are balanced, then pleasure and prosperity will inevitably be found.

CONTEMPLATION

It is night in a cemetery. A pile of stones sits in the quiet and darkness. In the perfect stillness of the night air, a rock dislodges itself and rolls with great noise to the ground. All is again silent.

DIVINATION

Correct judgment; full measure of all good things upon proper understanding of the situation at hand; a verdict of law that offers benefit, pleasure, and prosperity; the understanding of death gives one access to the pleasures of life.

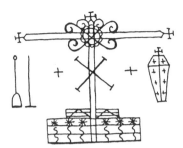

RADA • AIR
GUEDEH

Papa Guedeh
He is a fine fellow
Papa Guedeh
With top hat, tails, and one dark eye.

Lust's bright ember shines within the darkness of the grave. Guedeh rushes forth where angels—and for that matter demons—fear to tread. His step is light and apt to bring laughter as well as public revelations of a personal and often embarrassing nature.

The verse above describes typical Guedeh attire. His dress is worldly. His glasses contain one smoked and one clear lens. This graphically demonstrates that he sees with one eye into the Visible World and looks with the other eye into the World of the Invisibles.

The aspect of this card emphasizes the saturnine qualities of Guedeh's character. He sits pompous and reserved, his arms folded across his chest in a gesture of self-containment. There is little of the divine fool in this manifestation. Behind his sunglasses, his eyes seem to have turned inward to more closely examine the somber aspect of his realm. His solitary companion is a beetle, reminiscent of the sun at midnight, which crawls before him.

The primary attribute of this card is a deep introspection that focuses upon the night side of the soul.

CONTEMPLATION

It has been said that the adept laughs on the outside and cries on the inside. One must first acknowledge and accept the sorrow of existence and know well its boundaries; only then it is possible to transcend its territory.

DIVINATION

Sorrow of a deep and brooding nature; the joy and gaity that attends the release from this sorrow.

SANTERÍA • EARTH
OYÁ

Whirling cloth tears through worlds. Oyá, wild dancer on death's thin edge, the ancestors rise to your call as the jangling beat of bata guides your feet. Within you the womb and tomb are held in perfect balance. Mistress of the marketplace where all paths meet. Mistress of the Earth's deep, searing pressures. Mistress of the sky's hot fire. Sky's whirlwind tearing into Earth. Mother of Storms. All hurricanes in final reckoning bear your name.

In New Orleans, hurricane season is the time of Oyá. All of these storms are named for her sons and daughters. Her family is closely watched.

The power of Oyá celebrated in these cards is the elemental might of earth acting through Binah. She shares the Earth's power, compacted and ever erupting under the tremendous pressure. Her name itself is associated with a tearing. Among the Yoruba, it is she who owns the torn cloth used in the ancestral masquerades of the Egungun. She is also the patron of the women who command the marketplace.

Her aspect in this card is that of a woman dancing while covered with the torn cloth of the Egungun maskers. She holds lightning to illustrate one of her manifestations, that of Mother of Storms. The lightning of storms is hers, while the thunder belongs to Shango (Earth of Hod). She dances atop a tomb covered with a growth of eggplant, which is sacred to her.

A primary attribute of Oyá is tearing or a wrenching movement between worlds. As do the Guedehs and Brigitte, she stands between the worlds, although her movement between them has a more wrenching or tearing quality.

CONTEMPLATION

Lightning strikes a tree within the graveyard. It falls and becomes covered with the far-reaching growth of an eggplant.

DIVINATION

An abrupt change in a situation; gain in the marketplace; turn for the better in matters of business.

THE FOUR FOURS

CHESED

MERCY, BENEFIT

As Geburah is the vessel of severity of exact judgment, so Chesed is the vessel of mercy. Mercy is that state wherein strict judgment is not exacted. The self is expanded beyond the original parameters of a situation to include or enclose more variables than strict justice would deem appropriate. This elasticity, this flowing and enclosing, is one of the properties of water, which is the namesake of the loa of this vessel.

The marriage of the Tarot and the loa occasions shifts in perspective and viewpoint. Agwé is a loa of the sea; therefore the attribution to Chesed is apt and by no means forced. Within the symbology of the Golden Dawn, Chesed is the realm of the sea. Traditionally, Agwé is not particularly characterized as a loa of mercy; history has often cast him as the captain of an armed ship. But Agwé is a large and important loa. Our predicament simply means that some characteristics of this great sea loa will be emphasized to the slighting of others. If you bear this in mind, it is possible to serve this loa well.

Agwé protects sailors and all those who by their will or against their will travel on the sea. It is through his waters that one returns to Guinée, the birth land of the species, the ancestral home.

As the great loa of the sea or salt waters, perhaps his attribute of mercy is best epitomized by those Ibo who, when they were brought to the New World, chose to walk into the water in their chains at Ibo Point, South Carolina. They trusted that the waters of Agwé would carry them home to Guinée.

PETRO • FIRE
AGWÉ
LA FLAMBEAU

Agwé La Flambeau bubbles and boils as fire of water. The power of this loa is most visible in volcanic eruptions when the magma strikes the salty seawater, giving rise to vast and twisting columns of steam. Boiling seas heat the air. The gentle motion of the waves take on a roiling turbulence. The essence of Agwé La Flambeau is best expressed as steam. As such, this loa is tied to the breath of Ogoun La Flambeau.

The aspect of this card is that of Agwé's boat riding upon a sea of molten lava. The boat holds together under these extreme circumstances. It has been built using the strongest materials and the best labor.

A primary attribute of this card is quick and sudden change.

CONTEMPLATION
Fire and water joined give rise to the vigorous dance of air.

DIVINATION
Union of opposites, which may express itself as a marriage; the quiet

before the storm; the unexpected (as in fire and water giving rise to air); shifting emotions; unexpected shifts, safe haven constructed with much labor.

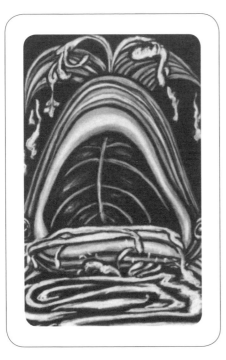

CONGO • WATER
LA BALEINE

La Baleine, the Whale, is water of water. She moves her body gracefully through the waters that gave birth to all. Her song unites the depths and heights of her watery world in a melody of creation and sustenance. She is the mercy of life incarnate. Hers is the soft sound of a great body as it parts the yielding waters. She is the vast world womb moving through the silent depths of the seas. She is a microcosm of the world, and as such knows great secrets. Her fins and her tail move her huge body between the surface, the airy portion of Agwé's kingdom, and the unfathomable mysteries of the deep sea orisha Olokun. Of Olokun it is said, "No one knows what lies at the bottom of the ocean."

The aspect of this card is that of a giant whale riding the surface waves. Her open mouth faces the reader and opens in cavelike shelter for those with the trust to enter. Much is gained through this trust; what is lost is a certain independence.

The primary attribute of this card is the protective maternal. The womb of La Baleine is a universe in which her children play.

CONTEMPLATION

A world free from care, in which all is provided.

DIVINATION

The gentle care of the mother; a desire to return to safe haven; a desire to nurture; overprotectiveness imposing unnecessary limits.

RADA • AIR
AGWÉ

Agwé is water or, more appropriate here, the elemental force of air expressed through water. The horizon where the sky falls to meet the sea is the point where these two elements join. This horizon is the point where Agwé's ship may be sighted. Between the waters and the sky his ship boldly moves. Deep below, where the waters meet the earth, he holds his banquets.

He is the lover of Erzulie in her form as La Sirène. As air of water and in relationship to La Sirène and Olokun, Agwé's primary point of manifestation is upon the water's surface. Of the sea trinity of Agwé, La Siréne, and Olokun, he is the most accessible. In that his ship floats safely over the waters, it is within his power to make the journey of sailors safe. He can promise safe passage. In terms of positioning on the Tree of Life, the ship of Agwé sails between the internal inspiration provided by the Master of the Head (No. V) and the worldly influences of The Market (No. X). One's fortunes may be safely entrusted to its hold.

CONTEMPLATION

A ship sailing upon deep waters, the land thousands of feet below its hull. The mercy of safe passage.

DIVINATION

Quiet in the presence of real or implied threat; trust that matters will turn out for the best.

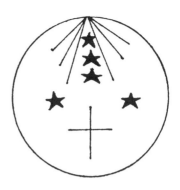

SANTERÍA • EARTH
OBATALÁ

Obatalá I see You on the Mountain
Obatalá I see You in the Sky.

Obatalá is the orisha of the white robe. The crisp white of the snow-covered mountain peak reflects this orisha's brilliance. The white clouds as they ride high in the sky sing Obatalá's praise names. As Nan Nan Bouclou is wise beyond knowing, so Obatalá carries within a profound and enduring wisdom. While Agwé's attribution to the vessel of Chesed requires an emphasis here and a de-emphasis there, Obatalá is a perfect fit for Chesed and the high qualities of mercy and largeness of spirit it engenders.

Obatalá is the father and mother of cool whiteness. The judgments of this orisha are as subtle as the mists that cover the early morning lands, and these same judgments are as strong and clear as the rays of sun that burn through the mists. Obatalá is the elder, the ancient, the ancestor. Androgynous in aspect and strong in years, this orisha is sometimes presented as male and sometimes presented as female. Obatalá is characterized by humor, coolness of mind, and equanimity.

Oba (King) Adefunmi I of Oyotunji Village, South Carolina, is an initiate of the mysteries of Obatalá. The impression that he gives is that of high initiation backed by humor, calm judgment, and generosity.

Persons with handicaps find a patron in Obatalá. The story goes that Obatalá became drunk on palm wine during the days of the world's creation and fashioned humans with handicapping conditions. To this day, the palm wine that brought on this drunken state is never drunk by those who dedicate themselves to the service of Obatalá.

The aspect of this card is that of a wise male elder. Snails, sacred to him because of their coolness, crawl on his arm. He is dressed in white, his color. Here is an orisha through which, in one of his aspects, the powers of the "elder male" can be honored.

His primary attribute is that of compassion and coolness. The road he walks is royal in the most exalted sense of that word.

CONTEMPLATION

Go back into time to a situation where your judgment was calm, forceful, and clear. Internally roam through the state that allows for such wisdom.

DIVINATION

Wisdom displayed in the matter at hand; fair judgment; correct assessment of a situation; mastery of a situation through calm, deliberate action; presents given as tokens of respect.

THE FOUR FIVES

GEBURAH

TECHNOLOGY, WAR

The four fives lie within the stomach of the vessel Geburah. This vessel is one of strict judgment, as its complementary vessel, Chesed, is charged with mercy. An eye for an eye and a tooth for a tooth captures the tone of Geburah. The loa and orisha of this vessel are apt to display fierce and warlike qualities, for this is the vessel of war. A warrior does not ask, a warrior takes what he or she wants (conversation with Zain, 1991). It is here that the aspects and attributes of those who grow to become warriors and soldiers are matured.

The warrior of Geburah has become in many ways outmoded. Modern warfare is no longer dependent on strong physique and determination of mind. One bomb can take the lives of millions, and the pressing of one button can launch that bomb. As the warrior of a hundred years ago is not the warrior of today, so the Ogoun of a hundred years ago is not the Ogoun of today. The loa and orisha exist in a complex relationship with the world; when one changes, so changes the other.

Along with war, Geburah is also the vessel of technology, in particular industrial technology. The technology of iron and massive metal constructions are particularly appropriate. Here also there is change.

To picture an Ogoun driving giant land-moving equipment is quite easy; to visualize an Ogoun at a computer terminal is a bit more difficult—at least for now.

The Ogouns live according to Western martial rhythms. The priests and priestesses of Oyotunji, an initiating village in Orisha-Voodoo, hold that the Ogouns are particularly important to the destiny of the white peoples. This village is committed to bringing Santería and Voodoo together.

For the most part, the fives point to problems and obstacles. Their appearance in a reading is apt to herald difficult issues, actions, or decisions. A general beneficial way of approaching these problems is to "cool" one's Ogoun. The spirits of this vessel live in all people, both male and female. At times they have, and should have, dominant expression, for there are situations where their fierceness is beneficial. However, there are even more situations where their fierceness can lead to a loss of advantage. Devotion to the spirits of Chesed, the fourth vessel, is a way to cool "Ogoun"; devotion to Obatalá is particularly effective.

One of the great tasks of the male voodooist in particular is to use the powers of this vessel effectively to the benefit of all. We could speculate that the defining qualities of male and female shift when the aeons shift. We seem to be moving out of one aeonic structure and into another. The qualities that made effective warriors in the past or old aeon are no longer as important.

These cards of Geburah have a certain split character. To repeat Darius James, "Voodoo does not exclude, it includes." The loa change. The Ogouns and what constitutes maleness are changing. This change is reflected in the descriptions given for the cards.

The more positive aspects of the fives point to an evolutionary development of these loa. The evolutionary or more evolved divinatory meanings are given in parentheses. The judgment of the reader and his or her knowledge of the question should decide which interpretation or divinatory meaning is used. If there is a question as to which meaning is proper, it is best to stick with the more traditional interpretation.

PETRO • FIRE
OGOUN
LA FLAMBEAU

Ogoun La Flambeau is fire on fire. Here the emotions burn at fever pitch. This Ogoun is characterized by dry heat like that of the desert. Given full reign, the forces represented by this card would pull the community and all within it into a dry mortal combat from which none would emerge.

The burning rage of Ogoun La Flambeau pushes him to take matters of life and death into his own hands. He may allow his rage to decide who will live and who will die. This usurps the position of the Guedehs; Guedeh will not take a man or woman whose time has not come. If Bon Dieu Bon has not declared the individual ready, Guedeh will not act.

This Ogoun has freed Haiti, he has fought in the homelands of South Africa, he has defeated Hitler. He is the power that drove the slavers from Haiti, creating the first black republic in the world. This Ogoun and the spirit of the Nordic berserker stand side by side. If not directed, his power could kill us all.

The aspect of Ogoun La Flambeau shown by this card is the soldier returning from battle. The fact that he is returning is most significant. This is not the soldier full of spirit rushing toward the battle, but the warrior who has seen Death's hand touch many. His sword has caught on the gristle as it cleaved through flesh. He limps; his leg has been wounded as an offering on the battlefield. Now tired, he sees that the battle is continuing and its pace has not slackened.

Ogoun La Flambeau has the honor of a soldier, tempered by the wisdom bought in combat. He knows that the price of maintaining this honor will be his other leg, then an arm, another arm, and finally his head. He is tired. Weariness shows on his face. His thoughts search for another way of "saving" the world and find no answer. They will find no answer until our species, asking the same question, finds an alternative to war.

The primary attribute of Ogoun La Flambeau is rage: the mad rush of battle, the singing of iron as it slices flesh.

CONTEMPLATION

Count your wounds after the Great Battle. Whose hand struck at you and at whom did you strike?

DIVINATION

Pain, especially physical; an aching questioning of one's actions leading to despair. War. Strife, internal or external. Actions against life and death must lead to regret. (Constructive use of a potentially destructive force. The ability to still question things and ideas to which one has given much.)

CONGO • WATER
OGOUN
BHALIN'DIO

O goun Bhalin'dio is iron, steel, and technology as healer. The fire and the force of this Ogoun is tightly channeled, directed by will much as a laser beam can be directed against disease.

Disease wears different faces. First, there is the disease that is given by Bon Dieu Bon. In this case, nothing can be done. The disease is laid upon the person as the will of God. Second, there are diseases that emanate from the Invisible World. They may be the result of an enchantment, call, or curse. A healer of the spirits, a mambo or houngan, can be of benefit in this case. A mambo or houngan can intercede with the spirits and can call a spirit down to give its advice in cases of this type of illness. A third type of illness is the result of the alignment of purely natural causes and chance.

The element of chance always is present. Eleggu á can jumble a message; Legba often speaks in riddles. Their advice can be misread or misinterpreted. With the third type of illness, the healing of Ogoun Bhalin'dio is paramount. The technologies and skills of the Invisible

World are used to treat the causes and symptoms of the diseases of the Visible World. With this third type of disease, technology is used to seek out and destroy the agents that occasion the disease's coming.

Most diseases are usually a combination of these three types in differing proportions. The proportions of the combinations decide the proportions of effective treatment.

The aspect of this card is of a determined healer. He holds a hypodermic needle in his hand. The needle rather than the scalpel is an apt emblem of this new Ogoun. In earlier manifestations, it was more common for this Ogoun to show himself as a surgeon using iron and steel to cut disease away. Technologies are now sophisticated enough to allow for less intrusive healing. The surgeon's scalpel is not the only recourse; perhaps in the not too distant future, this Ogoun will hold a laser. Ogoun Bhalin'dio is a true healer, an Ogoun whose field of battle is the inflamed body of the patient. Even in diseases where the cause lies in the spirit, these technologies are often necessary to ameliorate the symptoms.

CONTEMPLATION

The determination of the Healer. The combination of hot and cool qualities needed to combat disease.

DIVINATION

Trouble; worry; loss; possible onset of disease. (Recourse to or ability to act as Healer.)

RADA • AIR
OGOUN
FERRAILLE

Ogoun Ferraille, or Joe Ferraille as this loa is known in New Orleans, is the classic Man of Iron; in one manifestation, he is a blacksmith at the forge, with strong arms, the smell of sweat, and a leather apron. Ogoun Ferraille is the soldier in or at peace, as Ogoun La Flambeau is the soldier in war. His arms beat swords into plowshares.

Ogoun Ferraille is pictured here as a man of red-hot iron, joined with the molten materials of his trade. This card's air feeds the fires of the forge, whipping them to fury. Molten blood burns within iron flesh, giving rise to a shout that is more a venting of poorly contained steam than an exhaling of breath. This same fierceness allowed the enslaved people of the Ogoun cult to survive the Middle Passage.

CONTEMPLATION
Loss, even of one's own life, does not of necessity mean defeat.

DIVINATION
Loss, defeat, unfavorable outcome. (Bravery toward of certain loss.)

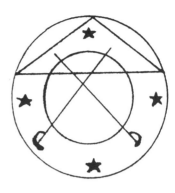

SANTERÍA • EARTH
OGGÚN

O_{ggún} is not a mercenary. His force of arms can be employed on either side of an altercation, but his loyalty cannot be bought. Oggún walks with those who call him. His might is that of the earth. A great rock pushed from the top of a hill does not distinguish among those whom it crushes. The might of Oggún is very much like this. Once called, directed, and released, the tremendous power of this loa may jump the predetermined channels of expression. Unforeseen shock waves can destroy all in their path.

Geburah, during the present aeon, is heavily associated with traditional male endeavors. Obatalá and Oggún are the two primary "cool" and "hot" aspects of the male character. Obatalá is cool, as Oggún is hot. In terms of conflict, Oggún is the warrior and Obatalá is the soldier. "Warrior" comes from the root word "war" and implies a violent, aggressive going forth. I once heard a voodooist remark that Oggún would rather fight his way through a brick wall than walk around it. This is the nature of a warrior. If a forest is an obstacle in a warrior's path, he thinks of burning the forest or blowing it to bits, rather than spending the time to make a detour around its perimeters.

Obatalá is a soldier. "Soldier" and "solid" share a common root in the Latin *solidus*; a soldier is one who stands solid in his beliefs, one who is not overly anxious to act. I am reminded of a story of Obatalá in which he is mistakenly imprisoned by Shangó. Obatalá sits patiently in jail until Shangó discovers who he is and makes profuse apologies.

It is important to realize that in the vast majority of cases the warrior Oggún can only show his power in the presence of and against the opposition of other males. While the soldier can stand solid on his or her beliefs against force exerted by a man or a woman, the violence of the warrior directed against a weaker foe quickly turns into rape, murder, and pillage, which both dishonor and defile his essence. If honor in this context can be measured as contending equally, there is no contest in the might of a warrior directed against a weak opponent.

Traditionally, war has perhaps been beneficial in that it has allowed the physically aggressive to enter into combat and greet death or victory. But modern warfare's violent surge moves to pull all—warrior and soldier, combatant, and civilian—into its iron and nuclear thicket.

The aspect of Oggún portrayed in this card is the power upon which civil authority rests. Oggún and Obatalá have joined in spirit to create this picture. Two police sit solidly upon horses, containing the flow of a Mardi Gras crowd. This is a depiction of Oggún, and for that matter civil authority, in its most benign guise. During Carnival, the New Orleans police are possibly at their best, and civil control is definitely at its most relaxed. Still, the police and the horses are quite formidable.

CONTEMPLATION

An iron gun, old yet capable of firing a lethal bullet. This gun was not made for target practice or the hunting of food. It has but one purpose. It has but one target.

DIVINATION

Containment of great internal or external pressures; stress; strain; worry that arises as a result of this constant pressure. (The strength to stand solidly before threat or adversity.)

THE FOUR SIXES

TIPHERETH

BALANCE, GOOD COUNSEL

In Praise of Legba

The Word is the domain of Legba. The Word is the ship on which Legba crosses the space between the Visible and Invisible Worlds.

Naming is an act of purpose and beauty. In the beginning, Legba danced and the stars fell from the heavens. They fell only a little way, for the heavens and the earth were not far apart. Legba walked among the stars, naming them.

The hot stars he called Virtue. He gathered them together and placed them in a large pot. There they sang their song and danced their frantic dance, giving freely of their heat to the airs that blow and encircle the Earth. This pot is the Cup of the Saints, and those who choose to drink gain a vitality of the Soul.

The cold stars he called Righteousness and strung them upon a necklace. This necklace he offered to Shi-Li-Bo Nouvavou to wear. The cold stars shook and glimmered upon her breasts, calling to all who would taste their pale fires. These fires confer a straightness and evenness of body and temperament.

In the beginning was the Word. Legba embraced the Word
and lay in its soft fullness to ride as a Chariot, as a Beetle, as
a Barque between the lands of the Spirits and the lands of
those who walk upon this Earth.

Sweet Legba, Son of Brightness, the sound of your cane
echoes in the emptiness between the Worlds. Your feet, fast
flying, part the ether and open the road. Walker on the
Crossroad, Caller of the Quarters, Giver of Names, Patron of
Beginnings . . . Bringer and Begetter of the Word.

—Martinié, 1988, p. 6

The vessel Tiphereth serves as a fulcrum of the Tree. It is a point
of balance, reaching out to hold the other vessels in place. In Tiphereth
seven paths intersect. This is the Court of Seven Sisters, the Point of
the Seven Powers, a reminder of the seven African tribes brought to
New Orleans.

According to Golden Dawn tradition, Tiphereth is the vessel within
which we can attain the knowledge and conversation of the Angel.
Among other things, this means that the occultist or voodooist who
has reached this vessel knows her or his place in the geography of the
spirit. The soul has expanded into the realms of conscience. Here we
hear the voice of our personal deity, the Master of the Head, the
Hierophant. Those who rest here develop a sense of what constitutes
right or wrong that goes beyond the dictates of cultural conditioning.
They reside in a timeless community, informed by the ranks of
ancestors who play ceaseless rhythms on their soul as one would on
the skin of a drum. Those who roam within this vessel can hear the
Word of their destiny within the interplay of these rhythms.

Tiphereth carries the powers of the Sun; here the great star moves
through its phases. Legba La Flambeau is the new or red sun. Shi-Li-
Bo Nouvavou is the sun at midday, and Papa Legba is the old or black
sun. This is the birthplace of stars, and Elegguá is the eternal child,
precocious in all things.

Tiphereth is the starting and ending place of all purely beneficial
magickal expeditions.

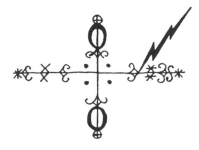

PETRO • FIRE
LEGBA
LA FLAMBEAU

Legba La Flambeau, as the new sun, unfurls himself in the heavens, brilliant beyond description. He revels in first powers, unweighted by knowledge of future consequence. His radiance stretches like a banner between the Visible and Invisible Worlds.

As this Legba dances at the crossroads, his dance speaks eloquently of the joy of creation. Here is a coming forth in victory. The gray hair and elderly visage of this Legba are emblems of his rank and show that even a new sun is the product of spiritual processes old beyond telling. Fire is will, and the fiery will of this Legba deeply penetrates the six directions.

The aspect of Legba La Flambeau is that of a newly initiated elder dancing in the crossroads. Fire shoots from his hands. His cane is a staff of fire, and his face wears a look of mischief. Although this look is devoid of malice, there is danger here. The fire of this Legba carries within it the disruptive potential illustrated by Courir Le Mardi Gras (No. XV). The sparks of this Legba's creation jump the vast emptiness between subject and object. He has no concern for where they land or what havoc they wreak. His will is creation pure and simple; in this he is sublimely successful. He moves between worlds with the snap of an electric spark. His feet crackle upon the ground in an ecstatic dance. The new or red sun burns brightly at his back.

Will upon will, fire upon fire fuels this frantic dance. His words are few and powerful. They seem to fall from his mouth pushed by an internal intensity that makes light of all external opposition. Just as there is great danger in calling this Legba, so there is also great danger in leaving this loa uncalled and unknown. His fire burns quickly through obstacles, those blocks to the unfolding of the universal will. Be certain that you are not one of them. Examine your actions carefully and approach this Legba only in the fullness of your will. When you offer him all, his fires open and cleanse.

The primary attributes of his Legba are success, victory, and ongoingness. What could stop a force such as this? What could stay the fiery hand as it reaches through the crossroads? Again, this Legba mirrors the Courir Le Mardi Gras. The force this Legba wields is beyond intellectual comprehension; it is untempered by compassion. He dances alone, fed by the awesome power of his own making. By his Word, he creates himself. Self-creating, his self knows no other.

This Legba dances on the head of the Pure Fool and the Enlightened Fool. A person guided by this card may be either of these two Fools. A key to discerning which one is applicable is the degree of stability or the ability to carry out a sustained action or effect. The Pure Fool may produce a brilliant display, but the effect is similar to that of fireworks in that it is of short duration. The works of the Enlightened Fool are much more likely to persist over time. This Legba is the force and fire of both fools.

CONTEMPLATION

Touch the newness in your soul that has never known defeat. The newness that has never strayed from its original purpose. The image is that of the mane of a young lion that has never been tangled or torn in the heat of battle.

DIVINATION

Victory, obstacles swept aside, the first necessary victories of the Pure Fool. A newly initiated elder flexes his or her first powers. "There is no grace: there is no guilt: This is the Law; Do what thou wilt."

CONGO • WATER
SHI-LI-BO
NOUVAVOU AND
DAN-I

Shi-Li-Bo Nouvavou signifies "initiated or loved by the sun. . . . This is the voodoo loa which alone unites the most magic forces . . . represents omniscience in voodoo" (Rigaud, 1974, p. 96). As the sun at midday, Garande is the emblem of secure power. She is the zenith of the solar force, assured and possessed of confidence that is tempered and strengthened by time and knowledge.

During the writing of this book, the loa Dan-i presented itself to me so well and so forcefully within the context of this card that inclusion is only proper. For example, in a recent dream Dan-i wore the aspect of a black man with strong albino characteristics. In this dream I went below the waters, and Dan-i came to me as a loa of possession and embraced me. Rigaud identifies Dan-i as a totally beneficent ancient loa who "sums up" possession (1974, p. 92).

In my own work with this loa (or more properly, its work with me) Dan-i revealed attributes that are identified with the light emanating from the night sky. The image came of a star snake or white snake stretching out upon the night sky much like a constellation or the Milky Way. The body of the snake created a path or a road for the ancestors to walk. Dan-i appears to me to be a distant star loa transmitting currents associated with the passage of ancestors through the night sky. Perhaps Dan-i wished to be included at this point to emphasize the connection between the light of midday and the light of midnight.

The aspect of this card combines elements of Shi-Li-Bo Nouvavou and Dan-i. A feminine Dan-i is pictured bathing in the fire of the sun.

CONTEMPLATION
The sun at midday, at its zenith, central to all.

DIVINATION
The joy of will manifest, the questioner's Work in its fullness.

RADA • AIR
LEGBA

Odu Legba, Papa Legba
Open the door
Your children await.

Papa Legba, open the door
Your children await.

—Call to Legba

Legba is the storyteller, and his tale is that of the procession of the suns through the day's sky. The blazing red sun of the new heavens announces his presence. The sun of midday, vast in power, blesses his going. The old sun, merged with the black of the night, tempers and tunes his wisdom.

Light creates as words create. Words and their naming are the light of the soul. They pull form from the fertile darkness. Legba is connection and creation, just as the Word is the means of connection and creation.

Papa Legba's words resound through the crossroads to those spaces where tales take on form and gently swing between the Visible and Invisible Worlds. The crossroads is the matrix of the web whose strands vibrate to the tale's telling. The mouth talks, the ear hears, and the soul sings the song of creation.

The tales of Legba have no ending; they grow from within. Their words and characters take on life, ranging afar; they send out roots, branches, and tendrils that twist and turn into unexpected shapes and reach into unexplored places. These are the tales that weave destiny.

The aspect of this card is that of a storyteller sitting at the crossroads. He is surrounded by children who sit in rapt attention. The black sun blazes behind him. The storyteller has seen much and has many tales to tell. The children have seen little and so contribute their silence to the tale.

The primary attribute of the card is the ability of the Word to make fertile the World.

CONTEMPLATION

The old tales, the old myths oftentimes carry within themselves more truth than recorded history.

DIVINATION

A task that may be accomplished through words. The door opens; obstacles are removed.

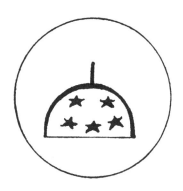

SANTERÍA • EARTH
ELEGGUÁ

Saint's head of concrete, Orisha of the jungle come to the city. Cowrie-shell eyes stare from behind doorways, from under objects. Hidden Elegguá, Elegguá the watcher, Elegguá the trickster. Concrete laugh from cowrie mouth. Followers of Santería often have concrete orishas hidden behind doors to the house to protect it. Some build buildings, some build saints. Ori (head) lost as shadows lengthen. Come play in the brightness of the sun.

As Legba is the old man who walks through the phases of the Sun, so Elegguá is the child who carries the Word and new seed to lands barren with age. Elegguá is the child orisha dancing between the red and black suns of Legba.

The aspect of Elegguá presented by this card is that of a young girl with cowrie-shell eyes standing partly behind a door. She is ever the trickster. She will let you in, but there is no telling whether you can get out. On this card, the door is open to indicate a clear path (success).

The primary attribute of Elegguá is that of playfulness. Messages entrusted to his care without proper sacrifice can often be jumbled.

CONTEMPLATION

A message given to a child to relay.

DIVINATION

Proper care in the matter at hand ensures favorable outcome, the influence of a child or childlike person.

THE FOUR SEVENS

NETZACH

EMOTIONS, VENUS

The four sevens are attributed to Netzach, the seventh vessel of the Tree of Life. The powers of these cards lie within the emotions. The Sevens trace the feelings and emotions through their elemental manifestations in fire, water, air, and earth.

The terms "hot" and "cool" are used in Voodoo to describe the essential nature of states and happenings. The emotions are in general hot, while the intellect and intellectual pursuits are viewed as cool. Hod, which is directly across from and balances Netzach on the Tree, is the vessel of the intellect. Netzach is a hot vessel, while Hod is essentially cool. No general value judgment can be made concerning the innate merits of either hot or cool characteristics; for both physical and spiritual health, it is necessary to balance hot and cool influences in one's life.

The full spectrum of the emotions finds expression in these cards. The word "emotion" is derived from the Latin *emovere*, meaning to "stir up" or "move out." These four cards very powerfully point in the direction of movement, particularly of an internal nature. Erzulie, La Sirène, and Oshún stir up attitudes and situations. They are like the steam that turns the great wheels of fate and destiny.

PETRO • FIRE
ERZULIE
LA FLAMBEAU

Erzulie La Flambeau burns with the fires of an overwhelming passion. Her rage rips at the fabric of existence. Erzulie La Flambeau is the torch that lights the way, burning through all resistance. She is the final resting place for all such emotions. In her heart they flower, and in her actions they are spent. Destruction often must precede construction. Sometimes the world and its things must be ground into fragments for the good to be freed. The dance of Erzulie La Flambeau is one of such grinding.

This grinding is an attribute shared with Erzulie ge Rouge. Erzulie ge Rouge means Erzulie of the Red Eyes. The eyes of this Erzulie burn like the torch of La Flambeau. In *Divine Horsemen*, Maya Deren speculated that Erzulie ge Rouge has syncretized attributes of the Carib corn deity, a wrathful deity who is as apt to grind people as she is to grind corn.

The card depicts a woman dancing upon and thus grinding ears of corn. Her dance creates food from raw agricultural products. She is the Corn Mother, and as such she is capable of creating the energy necessary to transform base products into foods. The transformation she effects is swift and violent. The air around her churns with the movement of her legs and the knives she holds.

A primary attribute of this Erzulie is fury. She is the berserker armored by Fury, equally capable of grinding corn or those who eat it.

CONTEMPLATION

Rage and hate binds you to your object as closely as does great love. Hate and love are both sides of the coin whose denomination is union; Will is the name of the Hand that distributes these coins.

DIVINATION

Forceful and decisive action in the matter at hand, bringing to bear the full force of emotional involvement in the situation; swift emotional ordeals leading to a refinement of personality or spiritual essence; rage; persons united by anger.

CONGO • WATER
LA SIRÈNE

La Sirène is the mermaid. While her realm is that of the ocean or world womb, her human qualities give her access to the mysteries of the land. She is the great bridge between those who inhabit the fathomless depths of the seas and the creatures of the dry land.

She is the water form of Erzulie, and Agwé is her husband. In terms of Chesed, she also acts as a connection or bridge between Agwé and La Baleine, the whale. La Baleine moves freely along the oceans' bottoms and is privy to their secrets. From her, La Sirène has much to tell Agwé.

La Sirène, as her name implies, is a loa responsible for the sacred songs of the Voodoo ceremony. These songs combine Music and the Word to generate the fascination that helps to so strongly focus the attention of the Voodoun devotees. Here once more, La Sirène bridges two elements; music and the spoken word.

Her card emphasizes blue, which is her color. The whale shown swimming behind her is La Baleine, the great Mother of the Sea. La

Sirène is companion to the whale and transmits the generative power of the oceans in the sphere of the emotions. She is a creature of two worlds, bridging the gap between the solid land and the ever-shifting waters.

The primary attribute of La Sirène is emotional connection. Her power is that of empathy.

CONTEMPLATION

We stand with one foot in the Visible World and the other in the World of the Invisibles. We operate as a connection or link between these worlds. La Sirène is the emotional component of this link. In her is found the emotional force to bridge this gap.

DIVINATION

In affairs of the emotions there is to be a bridging or a joining of elements. A marriage is the most obvious manifestation, whether the elements of the marriage are two people or a bringing together of ways in which the world is being perceived. The "siren song" of deception, causing one to forget his or her will.

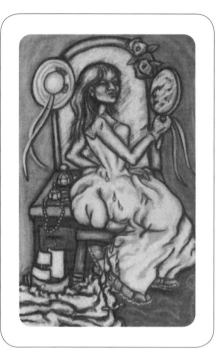

RADA • AIR
ERZULIE FREDA
DAHOMEY

Erzulie Freda Dahomey is the Erzulie who walks upon or governs air from the sphere of the emotions. The two reflecting mirrors in the card point with their fleeting images to the transitory and ever-shifting "airy" nature of the emotions. Wish is piled upon wish until the mounting pyramid of impossible aspiration vents itself in cleansing tears. The tears in the card form a body of water on which a ship sails. This is the ship of Erzulie, which promises to connect the emotional dream world of Erzulie with the profound creative principles embodied in the sea, the home of La Sirène.

Here, Erzulie is the virgin. By this is meant that she carries within herself a newness or freshness to experience. To be virgin is to be unmarked. One can experience the Carnival of the world in its entirety and still maintain a virginity as pure as any cloistered within ivied walls. Erzulie's freshness generates a readiness, a longing to experience all that the world before her has to offer. In a deep sense, the longing of Erzulie mirrors that of the Visible World for its invisible counterpart and that of the Invisible World for the joys of the physical.

In this card the emotions find no stability; they fly one over the other in a mad dash toward an improbable goal. Erzulie can move to that place where all is possible. She can choose the best of all possible worlds and glory in its unfolding; she can "conceive beyond reality... desire beyond adequacy" (Deren, 1953, p. 138). It is her curse to then awake and mourn as the golden radiance of what could be is lost in the dull light of others' constricted imaginings. Soft shadows soon fall prey to harsh light. This is the nature of the tears of Erzulie. Resolution is found in emotional catharsis. This venting provides a chance to link with powerful reservoirs of creative energy.

CONTEMPLATION

Board the ship of Erzulie. Stand upon its deck as it moves through the clouds and into the deep astral waters of the moon. Sails sheer as spiderweb unfurl to the night winds. Here all is possible. Desire is answered in the telling. Deep within, you know it is so.

DIVINATION

Imaginings beyond possibility, the jolt of shattered dreams.

SANTERÍA • EARTH
OSHÚN

Oshún is the Santería goddess of love. She is a patron of the earthy aspects of love as well as of art and dance. The emotions she expresses are deeply tied to the sacred earth.

As a deity of love Oshún shares many attributes with Erzulie, but there are no tears in her self-assured demeanor. She carries within herself the power of love firmly planted in earth's steadying influence.

This card pictures her with a fan (air) and mirrors (illusion), but she manages to look from the surface of the card squarely at the reader in an assured, solid fashion.

Her primary attribute is her ability to ground the emotions, to give them a solid form in which to reside and grow.

CONTEMPLATION

Take stock of your loves. Look at the ways in which they take on substance and form. This is one of the faces of Oshún.

DIVINATION

Emotions manifest in concrete fashion. A sacrament can be defined as an outward sign of an invisible or interior state. The creation of a sacrament which will bring to fruition some emotional involvement. For example, the purchase of a house can be viewed as an outward sign of emotional involvement in a social or biological family. Possible disappointment in the solid forms love takes.

THE FOUR EIGHTS

HOD

MAGICK, MIND

Within the eighth vessel of Hod, the mind and magick come together in a dance that leaves the practitioner spent, empty. Here the mind and its uses take on a new dimension; a fullness is discovered at the cost of what once was thought to be the bedrock of one's being. In terms of this deck, "Silver breaks rocks" (Deren, 1953, p. 288), meaning that the reflection of the silvered Magick Mirror (No. XVIII) has the power to break through the thickest of barriers—and, for that matter, heads.

The mind is an apt tool and an ill master (conversation with Nema, 1979). Generally we of the New World are taught to identify who and what we are with our mind and to define the mind as intellect. "I think, therefore I am" embodies this assumption clearly.

This is a trap of the greatest magnitude. If we in our "being" are our mind, and if what and who we are is contained within its far or close intellectual boundaries, then we are reduced to what we are able to think about, what we are able to know through the mind. Other animals have a sense of things not dependent on the intellect, a wildness that answers to the wildness of the world and allows for a participation in life more sure and immediate than that offered by the mind. "Instinct" is merely a term used by the mind trying to know this primitive (as in *primary*) "sense" of things.

Connaissance (profound spiritual knowledge) is a term used in Voodoo to include both this wild sense and the knowings of the mind. Voodoo does not exclude, it includes; all is conserved and put to use, and the mind most certainly has its uses.

The mind has been described as a Magick Mirror, taking in and reflecting all in the manner of its own nature. The mind first sees and interprets; then the interpretation affects the seeing. This, in the realm of magick, affects the thing seen. The Magick Mirror allows the mind of the magician to observe him- or herself. In using the Mirror, what is seen is purposely interpreted by the will, causing the image in the mirror to change. The image acts as a witness; it testifies to the nature of the change and can be examined by the voodooist. The change in the mirror causes a change in the voodooist, and the first steps of the expedition are taken.

Simbi and Shangó, the water snake of Voodoo and the proud king in Santería, find their home within the vessel Hod. Simbi is quickness, while Shangó is might. They are both great masters of magick. They know well the secrets and secret places of their realms. They both have enlarged their minds and enriched their intellects to yield the rich brew which is connaissance. The Western counterpart of Simbi is Mercury. Mercury, like Simbi, is a spirit that has great knowledge of magick. Simbi takes on the dual form of the Marassa (No. VI) on Mercury's staff.

Hod is paired with Netzach on the Tree of Life. They are as Marassa, Hod being the intellect, while Netzach brims with the emotions. Hod is air, while Netzach is water. These are the two elements crucial for life to exist on a minute-to-minute basis. We can live for a long time without earth beneath our feet or fire to warm us, but without water or air our stay on this planet would be quite short. Most important in terms of this Tarot, air is the nation of Rada, and water is the nation of Congo. Hod is air or Rada, while Netzach is water or Congo. These two nations, these two ways of being in the world, meet through the mechanism or path of Deluge (No. XVI). In Deluge there is an overflowing, a breaking down of barriers. Preexisting conditions fall before an onslaught of the primeval Waters.

Simbi manifests itself in New Orleans in a unique form. Voodoo rites often make use of Le Grand Zombi. This is a force called through a snake, at times a rattlesnake. Le Grand Zombi is the channel through which the grace of Bon Dieu Bon flows into the ritual participants. I believe that in the passage through New Orleans, the powers of Simbi became associated with the Zombi. There is a close similarity in the names Simbi and Zombi. Simbi is represented by a water snake, and most water snakes are poisonous; poisons of various kinds are also reputedly used in the creation of the Zombi. In New Orleans, the power that is Simbi rides within Le Grand Zombi.

PETRO • FIRE
SIMBI
LA FLAMBEAU

Simbi La Flambeau, bright torch, line of fire. Quick to rise above the heavens' clouds, quick to plunge beneath the earth's brittle crust, you seek the fire of fires that burns within. Tail of fire, body of fire, eyes of fire, tongue of fire.

Hod as the intellect is an airy vessel. If not held in check through the strength of Will and the direction of Love, the intellect and the thoughts it entertains are apt to swirl and rush in any direction. Simbi La Flambeau is fire in an airy vessel. Air feeds fire, brightens fire; fire feeds upon air. This loa burns with an intensity awesome to see. Within this card the Mind burns with a brilliance, an awful clarity that, if self-directed, often blinds the seer.

Simbi La Flambeau is the fire of the intellect burning through layer upon layer of illusion. In the pure heart of the flame lies the gate through which this Simbi finds egress into the Visible World.

The fires that push us to know are channeled in upon themselves, and bit after bit of knowledge upon knowledge is made subject to this fire and transcended. As Prometheus stole fire from the heavens, the fire of this Simbi is stolen from the emotions.

The creations of the mind represented by this card struggle for an otherworldly perfection. They are short-lived in the Visible World. The primary attributes of this card are instability and the mind as liberator; here is found the fierce determination of the mind to transcend its own creations.

The Simbi of air finds power in transcending the emotions. A coolness of judgment rides upon the even path of this transcendence. Simbi La Flambeau harnesses the emotions as one would a wild bull. Discarded ideas and truths fly as sparks from this bull's hooves.

The card shows a dragonlike Simbi La Flambeau swimming in the fiery rush of the emotions. This Simbi is ridden by a voodooist intent on plumbing these depths. She holds tightly to the snake in a form of sexual union.

CONTEMPLATION

Observe your thoughts. What part of you thinks? What part observes?

DIVINATION

Short-lived perfection; an uncovering of hidden motives or aspects of the affair at hand; secrecy with a tendency toward stubbornness; plots. Rapid thought or action.

CONGO • WATER
SIMBI D'L'EAU

Simbi d'l'eau, the water snake, whose green scales cut through clear water. Ripples splash dusty Time's foundation, releasing possibilities long held in its dry cubicles. Simbi d'l'eau, water's grand swimmer, you travel as a stream that winds through the land and cuts through earth's hard rock.

This snake of deep waters is able to travel through the deepest layers of being. As the whale La Baleine uses La Sirène as an intermediary to communicate with the surface, so Simbi d'l'eau whispers her secrets into the ear of the air or Rada Simbi. The Rada Simbi can then bring the knowledge to the mind's conscious attention. There is usually some distortion in this transmission.

This loa's watery nature connects the air of Hod to the water of Netzach. The connection is always posed in terms of a riddle. Simbi d'l'eau journeys from Hod through the path of Deluge (No. XVI) to the vessel Netzach (Erzulie, Emotion). The path from intellect to the emotions is best traversed not in dry declarative statement but in the wet, bubbling meter of riddle. For example: "What head has no mouth but still speaks? A drum."

This card's aspect is that of a large snake riding above the water. Its words appear in the form of airy Rada Simbis, which leap into the air in all directions from its mouth. This image refers to all the fabulous water creatures who broke surface to communicate their wisdom. These creatures traditionally promise much, yet speak in such convoluted riddles that mischief is almost assured if the hearer does not invest great effort in deciphering the riddle thoroughly.

A primary attribute of Simbi d'l'eau is a tendency toward confusion, marked by a sense of rightness or purpose without a firm idea as to how to translate that sense into concrete action.

CONTEMPLATION

A small stream cuts deeply into the land. Its darting waters disappear under a rock. The deeper the connaissance of the mind, the less in truth can be said.

DIVINATION

Correct impulse leading to equivocal action; a sense of the matter at hand which cannot be put into words; a breakdown of communication; falsehood through confusion, not malice. The sense of a confusing situation mishandled through lack of interpretative effort.

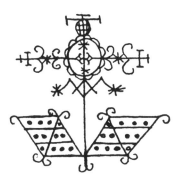

RADA • AIR
SIMBI

Simbi swims beneath the surface of the Magick Mirror, quick as a flash of light, still as the waves that constantly wash the surface of the mirror. A steady green water snake parts the surface of the mirror's mystery. Ears in the World of the Invisibles are listening to beginnings as yet unborn and endings of things as yet undone, as yet incomplete.

Quick, deadly, darting snake, sure traveler through light and dark, guide to souls as yet unborn. When you reach out from the depths of the mirror with quick head and quicker tongue, secrets that have been bound fast burst, become undone.

In the Zombi (No. XII) there are two snakes, both of which are identified with Simbi. One binds the Zombi's waist, while the other has taken on a threadlike form to sew the Zombi's lips together. The Simbi at the waist promises a possible release through magick. The Simbi that seals the lips shuts the Zombi off from the healing power of Naming. This illustrates that Simbi, or magick, works with both hands, for good or ill.

This card shows a spellworker surrounded by snakes. Bursts of light emanate from his hands to join with the air. He looks out at the questioner as from a mirror.

Magick is the primary attribute of Simbi. The magician is the molder of illusion.

CONTEMPLATION

Deep within the mirror there is movement, a darting, a quickening of the light. Deep within the mind there is movement, a darting, a quickening of the light.

DIVINATION

Magick used. Possible overapplication of force for, in contrast, a petty end. Complex means used when more simple would suffice. Unstable result (effects gained through magick tend to lack temporal persistence).

SANTERÍA • EARTH
SHANGÓ

Shangó: bright king, firm ruler, master of magick. Your kingdom resounds with the praise of your name. Spear in hand, feet on earth, you are invincible when facing enemies. Head in the air, seated on your throne, you are regal when helping friends. Great power and proud bearing carry you through the land.

In Guinée a great king once ruled. The flowers of victory, the flowers of wealth fell easily onto his head. He mastered the arts of ruling and ruled through the art of his mastery. His power was great and complete. He knew the arts of war as well as he knew the arts of magick. His actions ranged from beneficent to tyrannical.

Great power and accumulation bring jealousy. At one time his enemies massed, and his palace was burned down by lightning. Shangó went into the jungle and there, some say, hung himself. Others say that he ascended into the heavens. He passed into the realm of the Invisibles and, over time, became the great loa he is today. The cry of his followers is "Shangó does not hang."

The figure of Shangó is noble, and nobility is called forth by nothing so much as by tragedy. Tragedy propels nobility to its full measure. There is knowledge in his fall, and this knowledge gives rise to ascension. Shangó is the king become powerful, thrust from his worldly throne into the world of the Invisibles.

Shangó is the model of the mind risen to great heights that, walking in days of pride, stumbles over the thick growth of its own hubris. But the power of Shangó is that of the mind working through the earth. His is the grace not so much of creation as of administration. Through wise administration, the elements are arranged in such a way as to benefit all.

His tale contains a serious warning. In a coffeeshop conversation I was told that John Coltrane once said words to this effect: "When some have more than they need, then others are going to have less than they need." We are all parts of families, both large and small. If we prosper and our brothers and sisters do not share in our wealth, then the judgment of the ancestors will be upon us. To amass too much is to invite the retribution that flows freely through jealousy.

In this context, the story of Shangó can be interpreted in two ways. If he amassed too much wealth, then he took on the form of the Hanged man (Zombi) and underwent its enforced sacrifice. If he ruled in a wise fashion, then he went into the jungle, or deep places of the soul, and from there ascended to the heavens to rule with greater power and wisdom.

The primary aspects of this card are wise rule and adherence to family obligations.

CONTEMPLATION

When some have more than they need, then others are going to have less than they need.

DIVINATION

Family obligations fulfilled bring bounty to all; family obligations ignored bring destruction; wise rule; control of a situation used or misused. Excellent skill.

THE FOUR NINES

YESOD

TRANSPORT, MIRROR

Y esod is the ninth vessel of the Tree of Life. Within its sphere of influence is the Moon and all those shapes that call the lunar sphere of consciousness home. The territory of Yesod is the astral or high regions of the night sky. This is the first vessel on the Tree of Life to separate from the purely material experiences of Malkuth.

The magicks of Yesod are found in the glamour of the astral light. The card for the Moon is No. XVIII, the Magick Mirror. This is the mirror used by the Simbis of Hod, the eighth vessel.

Yesod is home to the Masa, those loa who are as tenuous as the astral light and as useful and necessary to our magicks as those forms the astral light generates.

The primary virtue of the Masa is transport. It is their function to carry water between one loa and another. The Masa flow between the points upon which the loa walk. These points can be viewed as convergences of energies that support the individual strengths of each loa.

PETRO • FIRE
MASA
LA FLAMBEAU

Masa La Flambeau, the torch bearers, are carriers of the molten liquids of the La Flambeau loa. The Magick Mirror begins as molten glass. Masa La Flambeau move and shape and still this fiery liquid. In this function they share the fire of the forge with Ogoun in his aspect as blacksmith. They are the kiln devils set by potters to watch over baking clay.

They preside over the physical creation, and thus the spiritual blessing, of all mirrors. Only they, through their art, are able to repair a mirror cracked during an expedition.

The aspect of this card is that of two furnaces and two male Masa. They carry pots of flaming liquid from one furnace to another. The furnaces are reminiscent of the two side pillars of the Tree of Life illustrated on page 24. The two pillars represent extremes of spiritual growth, severity and mercy. The Masa in this card transport the molten liquid in order to maintain a state of dynamic equilibrium between the two pillars.

Some attributes or virtues of this card are fiery distillation, a burning out of impurities, and the maintenance of balance through fiery transport.

CONTEMPLATION

Within every mirror dedicated to the art of magick, there remains a place that remembers its molten beginnings. To travel into the mirror to that place is to touch the heart of the mirror's power.

DIVINATION

Strong emotion bubbles under a calm surface. Hidden passion; rapid, unpredictable change; strength through balance.

CONGO • WATER
MADAME
LA LUNE

Madame La Lune walks in the waters of the astral light. She can grant use of the Magick Mirror. The firm waters of the Mirror, which catch and hold images, coalesce to form her wand or baton. Madame La Lune also shares in the Masa's function of transport by reflecting or transporting the light of the Sun.

The Mirror of the young Moon invites travel to soft places of the heart. Here the Madame is swathed in glamour. Soft filaments of light sway upon her smooth skin as the drums' mouths give forth honey. The powers or attributes here are those of enchantment.

The Moon at midcourse grows large or small, moving toward the birth of the full Moon or slipping into Night as the elder, cloaked Black Moon, which hides itself to drink more fully the nectars of the night much in the same way that Damballah and Ayida Wedo hide when they feed. The Black Moon shows Madame La Lune in her wisest and most secretive form. The Black Moon rides unseen upon the night winds. In this dark aspect, Madame La Lune is the Mother of Mysteries. She is the soul's black mirror. She has passed from this world into the world of the Invisibles, there to be refreshed and rebuilt by the hands of those who once constructed the pyramids and temples of the earth. As the Sun in its going from red to black, Legba traces the steps of Madame La Lune.

This card depicts a seated woman carving a moon, reflected by the water into parts or phases. The water has become a vast mirror upon which she can work the moon.

The primary attribute of this card is stability through change. The many faces of Madame La Lune come together to form a unified whole greater than the sum of its parts.

CONTEMPLATION
Stability through change.

DIVINATION
Cyclic change, a return to beginnings after a cycle is complete, orderly change. Enchantment, happiness.

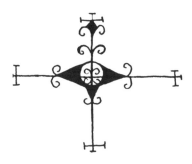

RADA • AIR
MASA

The Masa spin the star web that reaches between worlds. Delicately balanced upon its thin fibers, they carry water or grace from point to point. From the mercurial Simbi to the saturnine Guedeh, from Legba of the Sun to Azaka of the Earth, the Masa ply their skillful trade. They are the celestial go-betweens.

In the Masa's hands rests the virtue of connection. As bright lights they form the heavenly crown worn by Marie Laveau, another virtuoso in the creation of connections. As spirits or loa of air, they have often whispered their secrets into her waiting ears. In the economy of the Invisible World, it is the job or place of the Masa to carry power. While this power is not theirs to use, it is theirs to give. To carry power like they do, one must be able to transform oneself into a fit vessel as needed. The road from Legba to Azaka requires a different kind of messenger than the chasm between Damballah and Erzulie. It is up to the Masa to be all of these messengers.

The aspect of this card is that of a female Masa holding a teapot.

From the pot flow vapors that connect the pot, or Earth, to the stars. Z'Étoile (No. XVII) is the card of destiny. This Masa has indeed established a very important connection. A craft that has been created by the Masa to serve their function as go-between sails on the vapors.

The primary attribute of the Masa is transport. It is they who move the life-giving Waters.

CONTEMPLATION

In the dance of the soul, the burden and its bearer often become one.

DIVINATION

A move, such as change in residence, or the intercession of a courier. An expected gift arrives, for good or ill.

SANTERÍA • EARTH
YEMAYÁ

Great Mother, Our Lady of the Seas, strong mistress of sorcery and ocean storm, your feet trail softly over mist-drenched shores.

Yemayá is the power, the beauty, and the bounty of the oceans and all seawater. She is the tender mother who reaches out to protect her children. In her is found a distillation of the force of the Mother. She gives life and thus she can take life; yet she is forgiving, slow to punish even the worse neglect or abuse of her bounty.

The card shows Yemayá as a beautiful, pregnant orisha standing in the foaming sea. She is about to give birth.

The primary attributes of this card are fertility and bounty.

CONTEMPLATION
Honey flows freely from Our Lady's gracious bounty.

DIVINATION
Pregnant with idea or child; abundance; gain; a bequest of parental bounty.

THE FOUR TENS

MALKUTH

SOLIDITY, PRODUCE

Malkuth, your riches call to the Invisibles and draw them as birds to the seed, as bees to the flower, as moths to the flame. Great giver, great taker, great teacher, you delight the senses. The world in its unveiling lays bare the soul and its motives. All is caught and thickened here. Tenth vessel, blessed among blessed, you are the Visible World which supports and nourishes the loa. Feast upon feast and joy upon joy radiate from your rich soil. Toil and suffering unfold when this selfsame soil turns sour.

The tenth vessel is the domain of earth. It is here that fingers touch, eyes see, and the nose smells. It is within the realm of Malkuth that sensory information is harvested. Here the grace of Bon Dieu Bon solidifies and takes on physical form; aché, the blood of Olodumare, flows in a thick, visible stream. Azaka the poor farmer, the man of the country, is a loa of this vessel just as Ochosi is its orisha. Ochosi is the wild hunter. Gran Bois, the loa of woods, and in particular the Woods Below the Waters, is the watery spirit of this vessel. The farmer, hunter, and sacred woods join to sing the world's praise names.

In Malkuth is found the sorrow and joy of completion. The World of Day, the World of Night, and the shifting World of Twilight offer experiences that sound the lowest and highest notes of spirit.

PETRO • FIRE
AZAKA
LA FLAMBEAU

The flaming land reflects the flaming noonday sun. Fire clears the land and brings immediate usefulness, food for the stomach and charcoal for the fire used to prepare the food.

Azaka La Flambeau works hard. The fire of this loa eats at the fragile skin of the earth. The trees must be burned to make charcoal to sell and to cook food, yet if land stripped of trees falls away at the rain's first touch, where will the food grow? Too much has been taken. The fires reach deep into the Earth, leaving little. Haiti suffers, and we all grow to be less than we were, smaller, less able.

There is a desperation in Haiti and in the modern world in general which is understandable, yet extremely destructive. The future of the land is being destroyed so that we may eat meagerly today. Yet without food now, there would be starvation. The way out of this predicament is not a simple reversal of the initial path taken; the land is too poor, there are too many people. Some entirely new approach is needed.

The aspect of Azaka La Flambeau shown in this card is that of a dreamer. In the small fire of his pipe, two figures embrace in love to create new possibilities, solutions as yet unformulated and untried. The fire of this Azaka is sex and its ability to enflame the soul, projecting the species into the future against all odds. There is always hope, even in the most desperate of situations, when women and men can dream.

A primary attribute of this card is the grinding down of possibility. Bridges are burned before the land is reached.

CONTEMPLATION

If you can still dream, you can hope. If you can hope, there is a chance.

DIVINATION

Oppression, cruelty. Hope based on the ability to imagine a better situation.

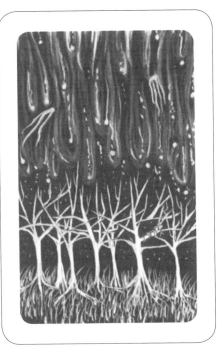

CONGO • WATER
GRAN BOIS

The domain of Gran Bois reaches from mountains to the Island of the Invisibles far below the water, far below the sea. This loa is master of the Sacred Forest. The trees of this forest have branches that reach past the sun in its shining and roots that tap the source of all waters.

The aspect of this card is that of the forest of the Island Below the Waters. This is the land the loa call home. This is the land to which the newly dead travel.

A primary attribute of this card is final favorable outcome. All is in its appointed place, and life gravitates toward the good.

CONTEMPLATION
We are composed of flesh and death, turn and return begetter of Transformations.

DIVINATION
Favorable outcome when the last words are said and last things done.

RADA • AIR
AZAKA

Country cousin, keeper of the nation's wealth in a simple macout (straw bag), your wisdom is won in battle against a dry and unforgiving soil. The easy riches promised by the Earth in its most fertile aspect lie just out of reach.

With hoe in hand and feet in field, you pursue the all-too-tenuous goal of survival. Such closeness to the Earth creates a knowledge of its less obvious gifts. Scarcity breeds a sharp eye. Azaka is a master of herbs, a healer who does much with little. His hospital rests in his sack. Its equipment finds form in his hands. His legacy is the Hoodoo Root Doctor. The term *Hoodoo* may be derived from "Voodoo" or "juju" (Haskins, 1978, p. 66). This doctor possesses a vast body of magickal practice, much of which centers around healing.

Strong sun on dry earth shapes the terseness of his character; words waste strength that could be invested in a deeper furrow. Bones ache, throat dries, what energy the land does not take goes to the blazing sun.

Cousin Zaca, keeper of family traditions. You who uphold the web of kinship trace ties back to the land, to those who sow it and lie within it.

This card depicts a farmer clad in blue denim walking upon well-plowed fields. In the form of the rainbow, Ayida Wedo offers her blessings. All is well now, but at any time conditions could change and the crop be laid to waste.

The primary virtue or attribute of this card is persistence in the face of nearly unsurmountable odds. Azaka is motivated by the constant threat of ruin. A failed crop could throw a struggling farmer into the nameless throngs of the city, stripped of family and the support it offers.

CONTEMPLATION
The earth as both healer and destroyer, taker and giver of life.

DIVINATION
Succumbing before the onslaught of inevitable forces, perseverance against great odds. Success at great price.

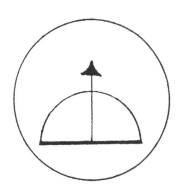

SANTERÍA • EARTH
OCHOSI

Ochosi, orisha of hunters and of the animals of the forest, the ground you roam has never known human step. Your sharp eye and sure hand provide food and clothing in the village.

The bounty of Ochosi is more than enough. This orisha provides what is necessary and more. The meats and skins must be treated and put to use quickly or they will be lost, rendered useless by decay.

The card shows a golden arrow shot into the bluish night sky and falling to earth. Blue and gold are the colors of this orisha. The stars (No. XVII) and the destinies they carry were the object of the arrow's flight. It found its mark and returns to the earth with its starry game.

CONTEMPLATION
Quiet forest morning. The sound of a bowstring snapping. An arrow takes flight.

DIVINATION
Accumulation; that which was gathered spoils if not put to use.

SIXTEEN TEMPLE CARDS

THE TEMPLE CARDS

COURT CARDS

For New Orleans Voodoo the royal road to Guinée, the African Holy Land, winds through Haiti. As the Haitian serviteur looks to Africa for inspiration and ritual form, so the voodooist of New Orleans looks to Haiti. Inspiration is like a well fed by diverse sources. The Spirits that inhabit the well's waters are the same for all. They may wear different clothes and require the use of different ritual items, but their essence remains the same.

The titles of these cards draw heavily upon an idealized organization of a Haitian hounfor, or temple. One of the strengths of Voodoo is its diversity of ritual and organization. The positions and the duties given for these cards are composite in nature, distilled from verbal, written, and experiential sources. They communicate the religious ambience of an operating temple; however, no one temple may or should be expected to contain all of these positions or roles.

The European Court Cards, with their King (Knight), Queen, Prince, and Princess, reflect a social structure or way of viewing the world that in Europe has been primarily secular for at least the last two hundred years. The figures on the Temple Cards of this deck move through an atmosphere more rarefied, more subtle than that occupied by the imperial figures of the Court Cards. Theirs is the world of religious expression rather than temporal power.

The Temple Cards of *The New Orleans Voodoo Tarot* make use of a sacred framework to embody those processes represented by the European Court Cards. Reflecting this sacred framework, the instruments of the hounfor are used instead of the elemental weapons of the suits. In this manner the pentacle becomes the calabash, the sword becomes the machete and crossroads, the cup is transformed into the serpent, and the wand becomes the drum.

During readings, the Temple Cards function to define two major areas of experience, the practical and the esoteric. In terms of practical divination these cards can be used to define certain physical and personality types. In an esoteric sense these cards point to certain spiritual influences likely to be found in the various personality types. The physical and psychological characteristics ascribed to each Temple Card are drawn from Robert Wang's descriptions in *The Qabalistic Tarot*.

The practical view afforded by the cards is very focused or narrow. When questioned, one point is brought to the forefront and examined in minute detail. The esoteric interpretation is more diffuse. Instead of the laser of practical divination, the reader sees a large amount of light as filtered through a lace curtain.

HOUNGAN

DRUM

KING, WAND

Houngan is a Dahomean word meaning "spirit chief." As a title it is not as widely used in New Orleans as its female counterpart, mambo. The title "Doctor" has a much wider use. The use of "Doctor" rather than "houngan" pays respect to the long-established New Orleans "Root Doctor" tradition. Dr. John (No. I) is an excellent example of a strong houngan.

Within the Temple's elemental dance, these doctors or houngans take the part of fire. As with the water of the mambo, fire both creates and destroys. The presence of water is much more persistent than that of fire. The same body of water can exert a force on its surroundings for days, but not so with fire. Fire comes, does its work, and then is gone. The drums of the houngan reflect the short-lived effect of fire. Drums can play for days, but they must be struck over and over again in order to produce their sustained effect. A fire may last for days, but its fuel must be constantly replenished. Water placed in a ritual basin or bowl persists much longer with no care.

The instrument associated with the houngan in this deck is the drum. This is done to honor the first Dr. John, to pay respects to the drum as a powerful religious instrument, and to mirror the houngan's fiery elemental attribution. In Haiti the houngan seldom plays the drum. In New Orleans it is much more common for the houngan or Doctor to be a drummer.

It is said that the ears of the serpent were the first covering of the drum. This points to the connection between the drum and the root creative processes of Damballah and Ayida Wedo. The rhythms the ritual drums create are not so much heard as felt with the whole body. Snakes have no ears, but they respond to the rhythmic vibrations created by drumming.

The drum is a sacred instrument. It combines elements of the plant and animal kingdoms in that it is constructed from the skin of an animal and the flesh of a tree. The drum has a head, a body, and a mouth. The head of the drum is washed and consecrated much as is the head of a voodooist. The drum is ritually fed through its mouth. Objects can be hung on the body of a drum to help focus its calling of the loa.

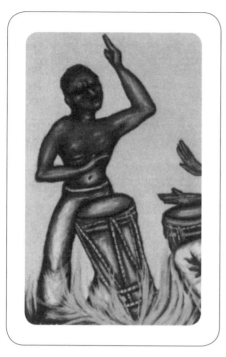

PETRO • FIRE
HOUNGAN

The houngan of fire represents the fiery part of fire. His is the virtue of fire doubled back upon itself. It burns with great intensity but is easily exhausted if other elements do not come into play. It has but one course, and that is to burn straight through. One of the Ogouns, perhaps Ogoun La Flambeau, shapes this personality.

This card shows a houngan playing a drum of the Petro Nation. The roping system used to secure and tighten the drum head identifies this type of drum. Fire issues from the mouth of the drum. This drum is like a hollow tube used to bring down the fires of heaven, a parallel to the story of Prometheus. The Petro rites challenge the established order of things just as that Greek hero did.

The character traits associated with this card include fierceness, pride, and impulsiveness.

Physically such a person is likely to be a man with blond, red, or reddish-black hair and blue, hazel, or light-brown eyes.

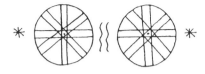

CONGO • WATER
HOUNGAN

The houngan of water is the fiery part of water so the personality of this houngan can show intense physical or mental involvement. However, the overbearing influence of water leads to a general passivity and openness to influence. The Masa may inform the personality of such an individual.

This card shows a houngan of the Congo nation drawing water from the head of the drum that then covers the surrounding earth. This illustrates that the houngan drummer provides a service and a blessing to all that is greater than the benefit he receives. He can only receive benefit equal to service rendered if he identifies with the whole of the hounfor congregation.

The character of the person aspected by this card is generally passive, idealistic, and given to the imaginative imagery used in poetry. He can be enthusiastic, but the enthusiasm easily falls away.

Physically this person is inclined to have light brown to blond or brownish-black hair and blue or light brown eyes.

RADA • AIR
HOUNGAN

The houngan of air is the fiery part of air. This is the stormy tempest of the heavens. The winds shake the earth to its foundation, and in the skies the clouds tumble one over the other. This houngan knows the value of swift attack. Shangó may well be the informant of such a personality.

This card shows a houngan playing a Rada drum. A distinguishing characteristic of the Rada drum is the pegs used to hold and tighten the head. The pegs can be likened to sunbeams issuing from the head of the drum. The Rada nation has been called the Golden Tradition due to its peaceful character and beneficent emphasis. The houngan has gone into possession, leaving the Visible World for that of the Invisible. His presence has a regal quality much like that of the great king Shangó.

Character traits of individuals covered by this card include courage, swiftness, and readiness to attack.

Physically the individual is likely to have dark brown or black hair and dark eyes.

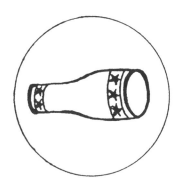

SANTERÍA • EARTH
SANTERO

The Santero (a male Santería initiate) of earth is the fiery part of earth. The fire of this Santero is the dynamic force that supports the growth of all the Earth's bounty. Fiery or extremely active disturbances of the Earth are also within his province. The fire of volcanoes and earthquakes are within his realm. Olofi may be one of the orisha who mold such a character.

The aspect of this card is that of a Santero making an offering of herbs to the Bata drums. The Bata are sacred drums of Santería used to call the orisha. The drums themselbves are hourglass-shaped with one large and one small head. Both heads are hung with bells around their rims. The atmosphere is one of sanctity and grace. Aché, the life-blood of the universe, flows freely.

Character traits of individuals covered by this card include a strong sense of the holiness of the Earth, which leads to patience and industry in physical matters (these traits differ from those described in the Thoth or Golden Dawn Tarot).

Physically, this man is liable to have dark hair and dark eyes.

MAMBO

SERPENT

QUEEN, CUP

The voice of Marie Laveau speaks from many throats. Madame L was the mambo supreme. In her dance with the spirits, she spoke with authority and power. She gave and she took in correct measure, balancing benefit and obligation. Her mercies and her rages are the stuff of history. From her throne on Congo Square to her ritual space on the Bayou St. John, her connaissance was acknowledged and deferred to. She stands as a model or standard for the chief Voodoo priestess of New Orleans.

Within the sacred elemental dance of the hounfor, the mambo is water. Water is that element that both levels mountains and cools the fevered mind. It is also the element used to call the loa. The drums (Houngan cards) are also used to call the loa, but water or the Water Road has a stability that the quick-fading sound of the drum lacks.

The mambo works with the serpent in calling the loa. The serpent is associated with the wet, moist aspects of human experience. The serpent is sinuous; all hard muscle and grace, it glides over the ground or moves through the water. The serpent is wild; it cannot be trained, only worked with. It swallows its prey whole with its large cuplike mouth. The snake represents the union of male and female, which speaks to Aleister Crowley's vision of the Queen (mambo) carrying a fertilized egg within herself.

In New Orleans Voodoo, the priestess or mambo generally has strong enough contact with the loa to enter into the mental state necessary to draw power from the snakes. The priestess and the snake is a pairing of tremendous antiquity. Rose, a priestess committed to developing a deep intellectual and experiential understanding of the African Mysteries, dances with very large and powerful snakes. Another priestess, Muslima Moonpaki, wraps the snake around her forehead in order to gain close communion with the spirit the snake contains.

PETRO • FIRE
MAMBO

The mambo of fire is the watery part of fire. Water controls fire, and this mambo has authority over the fiery element. She has united with fire and thus has the powers that come from knowing its secrets. Simbi La Flambeau may well have helped to shape such a person.

The card shows a mambo uniting with a fiery red snake. The snake has risen from the blood-red, molten river that flows by their side. Fire flashes between the head of the mambo and the Serpent as they exchange a breath of flame in their mutual ecstasy. The pleasure of the mambo in receiving the secrets of fire is matched by the joy of the serpent in imparting them.

The individual described by this card exhibits authority, a magnetic kind of attraction; she is generous in friendship and love, where she is apt to take the lead.

Physically this woman may have red, gold, or reddish-black hair, and blue or brown eyes.

CONGO • WATER MAMBO

The mambo of water is the watery part of water. She reflects and transmits images and occult impressions. She so easily and perfectly reflects all around her that her own image is nearly imperceptible. The Masa are the loa who probably have a hand in the forming of such a "head."

This card shows a blue snake wrapped around the mambo's waist. Water rushes from her hands, and she seems to be enveloped in a flow of water which takes the form of her hair. She wears a blue dress. The image of the water and the image she presents are mixed and almost inseparable.

She has a dreamy and tranquil personality, which tends to express itself poetically.

Physically she is likely to be a woman with black or brown hair with a golden hue, and brown or blue eyes.

RADA • AIR
MAMBO

The mambo of air is the watery part of air. Water thickens air and allows it to transmit larger amounts of both physical and astral information and power. Moist air carries sound and odors more efficiently over longer distances. It has been suggested that the strong affinity of New Orleans for the occult is due to its intimate association with the waters surrounding it. The rains and floods which inundate the city are extreme by any standard, and sizable sections of the city would be under water if huge suction pumps were not working night and day. The watery nature of the air makes it better able to carry sound, smell, and occult impressions (conversation with Bud Finger, 1991). This card has a strong resonance with the city of New Orleans. Ayizan is a fitting loa for such a personality.

The aspect of this card is quite striking. A mambo dances while holding a severed male head aloft. Her other hand holds a sword, and a snake is wrapped around her head. The virtue of this card is the sure transmission of perceptions. This card allows for accurate appraisal of a situation at hand through the clarity of these perceptions. The severed head held by the mambo represents illusion or faulty perception; the sword has been used to isolate illusion and render it harmless. The snake is entwined around the mambo's head much in the manner of the tignon (scarf hat) tied in seven points and worn by Marie Laveau. The serpent guards the purity and correctness of the mambo's perceptions. In Voodoo, important spirits ride within the head (see No. V, Master of the Head). If these spirits have been corrupted by magick or harmful actions on the part of the voodooist, it may be necessary to symbolically remove and reseat the head.

The character of the woman aspected by this card shows the traits of individuality, keen observation, subtlety, and accuracy of perception. She is graceful and loves dancing and any physical activity that involves balancing.

Physically this woman is likely to have grayish hair and light brown eyes.

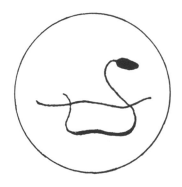

SANTERÍA • EARTH
SANTERA

The Santera (female Santería adept) of earth is the watery part of Earth. She is the ruler of earth and its watery, life-giving forces. In that she controls the forces of life, she also has great knowledge and control of the forces of death. In the past, the earth was viewed as passive and accepting; now it is known that the earth is an active, complex organism and accepts only so much before asserting itself with great force. The presence of Oyá or Obatalá should be considered in the makeup of such a personality.

The image of this card is of a Santera sitting at the edge of a vast swamp. A snake comes out of the watery earth and stretches up to her waiting hand. The swamp is filled with the forces of life and death, much like the Great Sea of Binah (The Four Threes). All potential is here. The snake may carry life or death.

The personality of such a woman is characterized by affection and a large capacity for the giving and receiving of love. Dire are the consequences if her love and loyalty are betrayed.

Physically she is likely to be a woman with dark hair and dark eyes.

LA PLACE

CROSSROADS AND MACHETE

PRINCE, SWORD

With bright blade lifted in salute to the temple and the spirits it contains, the la place dances with the machete to guide the movements of the banners. These banners are the symbol and sacrament of the temple's solidarity. Around the temple and its environs, the la place carries his machete and the hounsis bear the banners in a rhythmic procession, approaching objects and persons of special grace in praise and respect. The la place is a master of ceremonies whose duties include the overseeing of myriad ritual accoutrements and details.

The la place is the understudy of the houngan and may be preparing to lead the Temple's congregation. A woman in approximately the same position as the la place is known as the Mambo Caille, or "mistress of the house."

Within the sacred elemental dance of the Temple, the la place holds the position of the element air. The machete or sword is the instrument associated with the intellect in Western occultism. Its flashes are reminiscent of the intellect's mental flashes. In Voodoo, its virtue is that of Ogoun the Blacksmith, with all the rich connections between the forge and magick.

In the context of this Tarot, the la place is also associated with the crossroads, which signifies the connection between the Visible and Invisible Worlds. One of the functions of the machete is to clear the way for the spirits. It is as if the machete clears the road to the door that Papa Legba opens. This door can be symbolized by the crossroads. The four cards all contain representations of the la place or Oriaté wielding his machete over a crossroads.

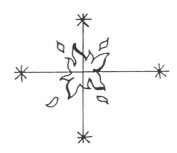

PETRO • FIRE
LA PLACE

This la place is the airy part of fire. Air feeds fire, causing it to grow and flicker wildly. Strength and swiftness are moral qualities that mirror these effects of air on fire. This la place is able to see both sides of a question and is a just man. Legba La Flambeau is well suited to this type of person.

The card depicts a la place drawing a crossroads of fire with his machete. As he traces the crossroads in the earth, fire leaps out of the cut. One hand is held aloft and one is pointed downward to indicate "As above, so below." He is bringing the fires of the upper atmosphere down to create a crossroads or gate between the Worlds of the Visible and the Invisible.

Personality traits of this card include nobility, strength, swiftness, and fairness of judgment.

Physically the object of this card is apt to be a young man with yellow or brownish-black hair and blue or gray eyes.

CONGO • WATER
LA PLACE

The la place of this card is the airy part of water. His is the power of steam to wield in the world. The pressure from steam is useful if controlled but, if allowed to build unnoticed, has the potential to do great harm. An Ogoun would be indicated as the source of this type of expression of personality.

The aspect of this card is that of a la place pouring water from one hand onto a sword he holds in the other, splitting the falling drops in two. The reference here is to the crossroads as splitting the world into the Visible and Invisible domains. The pool of water that has formed at the center of the crossroads reflects or mirrors the la place. This mirroring describes a relationship between the Visible and Invisible Worlds; one mirrors the other.

Characteristics of the personality described by this card are a calm surface covering a fiery interior, subtlety, secret violence, and craft.

Physically this card describes a young man with brown or brownish-black hair and gray or brown eyes.

RADA • AIR
LA PLACE

This la place is the airy part of air. The instability of air is magnified twofold. The intellect wanders from one subject to another, from a set intellectual position to its opposite. It is as if the mind is blown about by the winds created by its own prior movements. This creates a type of perpetual motion with no firm object or destination. The type of mind described by this card is highly intelligent but lacks firmness. Simbi may be an apt loa for a person with these characteristics.

The aspect of this card is that of the la place standing over the center of the crossroads. A golden whirlwind issues from the tip of the machete as it cuts through the air. It seems as if a great deal of show and power has been expended for minimal effect.

The persons described by this card are brilliant in argument and intellectual discussion, but lack conviction. The points they make so well are unrelated, one contradicting the other.

Physically this person is apt to be a young man with dark hair and dark eyes.

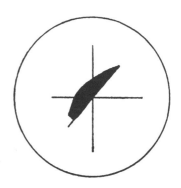

SANTERÍA • EARTH
ORIATÉ

An Oriaté, a priest who is expert in the Lucumi (another name for Santería derived from a Yoruba greeting used in Cuba meaning "my friend") prayers, is the airy part of earth. This Oriaté has great skill in bringing practical matters to fruition. Oshún, an orisha of herbs, could be one motivating spirit for such a personality.

The aspect of this card is an Oriaté pulling a sword (iron) from the concrete head of Elegguá. The reference here is to the Western story of Excaliber, in which a young man pulls a sword from a stone to prove himself worthy of being king.

The person associated with this card is apt to have a character that is competent, trustworthy, and reliable. He makes a good worker or manager.

Physically the person described by this card is likely to be a young man with dark brown or black hair and dark eyes.

HOUNSIS

CALABASH

PRINCESS, DISKS

Wine skirts swirl in greeting to the Spirits. Voices are lifted in song to ease their coming. The hounsis are the chorus, dancers, and suppliers of the Temple. Hounsis means "spirit wife" and refers to the deep relationship these members of the congregation enter into with the loa.

The work of the hounsis solidifies the sacred elemental dance of the temple, or hounfor. They act as the element of Earth. If the houngan, mambo, or la place can carry out spiritual work of a higher order it is only because they stand upon the shoulders of or are supported by the hounsis. Without their diligence, without their attention to the numerous physical requirements of ritual, the temple could not function.

Treated as spiritual children of the houngan or mambo, the hounsis are likened to, in a popular phrase, "leaves upon a tree." There is within this scheme a reciprocity that channels the flow of obligation and benefit both up and down the temple hierarchy.

The instrument of the hounsis is the calabash in its many forms. A calabash is a dry, hollow gourd that can be used as a container or receptacle. The calabash has numerous sacred functions. The Star (No. XVII) is likened to a calabash that carries our destinies through time and space. Ifa, the great oracle of the Yoruba, uses figures called odu to advise and council the questioner. The connotation of *odu* is "big calabash" (Gleason, 1973, p. 11). The assan, a gourd rattle covered with beads and snake vertebrae, is a high religious instrument and sign of rank for the houngan or mambo in parts of Haiti. The human body is very much like a calabash in that it has the distinction of being filled with various spirits at various times. In the cards, the four hounsis are pictured with four hollow containers, which are extensions of the calabash.

PETRO • FIRE
HOUNSIS

The hounsis of fire is the earthy part of fire. Her attributes mirror the fiery characters of the La Flambeau loa. As the earthy part of fire, she works to create the conditions proper for the La Flambeau loa to manifest themselves. Her character is a fit receptacle for these loa of flames.

The aspect of this card is extremely fiery. A hounsis holds a flaming zin, a ritual pot made of clay or iron that is used for cooking. The pot in the card seems to be of iron, so it can handle the tremendous heat of the flames. Brulé zin (boiling pot) is a ritual in which a hounsis makes Kanzo, that is, demonstrates mastery over fire. The hounsis in this card presents a spiritual vision of this mastery. She has united with the essence of the fire.

Character traits associated with this card include all intense states such as anger, love, ambition, enthusiasm, and vengeance. Her emotions are prone to rapid change.

Physically she is apt to be a young woman with gold or red hair and blue or light brown eyes.

CONGO • WATER
HOUNSIS

This housis shows the earthy part of water. She demonstrates the most gracious, kindest qualities attributed to Erzulie. She walks through a world filled with beauty. Flowers open and mouths close at her approach. Erzulie Freda may well work through this type of person.

This card shows a woman providing a spirit with entrance to the safe abode of the govi. A govi is an earthen vessel used to house loa or the spirits of the dead. The Waters swirl and rush into the mouth of the govi, which the woman has opened. A spirit, perhaps that of her now-dead husband or love, looks out from the entrance to the govi. Their romance can now continue, though on a different plane.

The character of the person identified with this card is dreamy and sweet. She is the great romantic.

Physically she is a young woman with brown or black hair and blue or brown eyes.

RADA • AIR
HOUNSIS

The hounsis of air is the earth of air. It is she who brings the amorphous driftings of air down to earth and gives them form and solidity. She takes the dreams of Erzulie Freda and the plans and strategies of Shangó and gives them a physical reality.

The aspect of this card is that of a hounsis caring for the Pots de Tête. These are earthen jars that hold the Ti Bon Ange (No. XIV) or Will of the voodooist for safekeeping. The human body and the Pots de Tête are both receptacles for the loa. This hounsis looks after the welfare of the jars in a protective and careful manner.

Character traits of individuals covered by this card include wisdom in the handling of material affairs, ability to translate dreams into physical reality, firmness, and aggressiveness.

Physically she is apt to be a young woman with light brown or brownish-black hair and light brown or blue eyes.

SANTERÍA • EARTH
YAGUÓ

The yaguó, initiate in Santería, holds the position of the earthy part of earth. Hers is the strength of the planet to support and, if needed, direct the forms of life upon its surface. The character of this yaguó is well suited to the indwelling of the orisha Yemayá.

This card shows a yaguó holding a pot and working with her Guerreros, or warriors: Elegguá sits by the door and looks out at the scene; Oggún is represented by the pot itself; Ochosi is an iron crossbow; Oshún is represented by an iron rouster on an iron cup that is attached to an iron pole. The warriors are all present.

Character traits associated with this card include benevolence, strength, beauty, and fearless protection.

Physically she is a young woman with blue-black, rich brown, or red-brown hair and dark eyes.

THE CARDS
IN PRACTICE

RITUALS FOR USE
WITH THE DECK

First you do the Working, then you do the work.

—conversation with Zain, 1989

In ritual, who we believe we are unwinds much like the spring of a clock. Our identities are then reset by the adept hands of the Mysteries we call into ourselves and into our ritual environment. The ultimate purpose of this Tarot is to assist both the curious reader and the confirmed voodooist in exploring or deepening their relationship with the loa. These rituals are well suited to this purpose but by no means necessary for everyone who wants to use the cards. To perform the rituals is to engage in a grand tour of the Mysteries' invisible world. Through the rites, the new practitioner is introduced to some of the major locales of the Mysteries' environment. The seasoned voodooist will find that the rituals involving the cards shed new light on old friends.

It is my experience that the loa most often tell you what is necessary to get a job done or situation remedied. They tell you where your effort is most effectively expended. First you do the Working (rite), and then you do the work. These rites have very little to do with quick and easy solutions. Ritual is not easy. It is certainly not something for the indolent. If the rites are performed for material benefit, the mental concentration and physical preparation involved can be more time-consuming than simply finding a more conventional means to obtain that benefit.

If you are new to the use of ritual, the underlying process is simple. To begin, it is best to engage in a willing suspension of disbelief, a state in which all doubts and reservations about the effectiveness of ritual itself are held at bay through an act of will during the time of the ritual activity. If the actions, sights, and sounds of ritual are far removed from an individual's everyday activities, then the practice of ritual may seem fantastic and foreign in the extreme. The question "How can I be doing this?" destroys the concentration necessary to begin the ritual activity.

The conscious mind is very good at questioning the validity of our activity, and these questions are valuable outside of ritual space. While performing ritual, it is best to be focused and totally directed toward the ritual activity. If doubts or questions should arise over the effectiveness of the ritual itself, simply allow them to pass through you and continue with the rite. Call upon the wisdom of Scarlett O'Hara and her "I'll think about that tomorrow" gambit. Give up your momentary concern in order to gain the advantage of fuller concentration. While the effectiveness of the ritual can be questioned and judged after the performance of the rite, an ongoing questioning attitude toward the manifestations of the ritual is important. "Are you getting what you called?" is a good question to keep in mind. If an older man were to appear in the Magick Mirror (No. XVIII) and announce that he is an Erzulie, I would certainly question any advice or directions he gave me. A sense of wrongness about a rite should always be heeded.

The willing suspension of disbelief should be applied to questions that arise about the effectiveness of ritual itself. The manifestations of ritual and their consequence to you and others can and should be questioned as a part of the ritual's ongoing process.

The underlying procedure of these rites is similar to that of most ritual work performed in any system (conversation with Delphine, 1982). During the rite, there is first a period where power is accumulated, a means for focusing that power, and a method for releasing it. Accumulation of power is closely tied to mental concentration; focus is a matter of narrowing the attention to the object of the ritual; and release is achieved by a sudden, and at times jarring, letting go of power. This is the underlying unstated structure. During any particular rite, when one of these three phases begins or ends is up to the temperament of the individual practitioner.

The practice of passing an object or food through the crossroads is found in a number of the rituals. This practice is simple and very effective in sanctifying the object or food. While using both hands to hold the item, draw a crossroads with equal arms in the air directly in front of you. Pass the item through the center of the crossroads with a throwing motion. In executing this throwing motion the item should leave your grasp for an instant. It is during this instant, as the item passes through the center of the crossroads, that it is sanctified.

These cards can, of course, also be used for workings that are malicious or whose intent is to control another. Power is power; it can be employed for any deed or end the practitioner desires. The caution here is simple: What goes around must come around. What you send out will come back to you. Your fingers will pick up stains from the pots you stick them in. Ultimately, it is up to you to decide the worthiness of any particular working. Choose well.

There has never been a deck quite like this before, so there have never been rituals quite like these. The use of the cards is new; the loa of Voodoo thrive on that which is added, that which is new. These rituals and practices draw heavily upon the work described by Mishlen Linden (1991). The potential for the development of additonal rites is limited only by the depth of contact the practitioner establishes with the spirits. Marty Laubach, a teacher and practitioner, uses mirrors in his workings that reflect one another to a seeming point of infinity. This technique is strong and deserves further exploration. The Black Moon Publishing Archives contain manuscripts describing additional rites and practices that may be adapted for use with this deck. Something begins here. May it in all ways have the blessing of the loa.

RITUAL TO HONOR THE VOODOO

The following rite can be used to bring the practitioner closer to the spirits. The loa or forces this rite honors are the Marassa, Legba, the Ancestors/Dead, and the Mysteries. It creates an esoteric hounfor.

The precondition of any existent thing is duality. "Is" as opposed to "is not" lies at the core of all existence. If the universe were constructed of one fabric, we would be so immersed in its fibers, such a part of its weave, that the cloth itself would be invisible to us. It is in duality, through difference, that we perceive the world. This is the domain of the Marassa (No. VI). The Marassa, the Twins, are not really loa. They stand apart. They are the holy conscious process that gives rise to the phantasmagoria of the Voodoo pantheon.

This rite is arranged to create a universe or sphere of understanding in which the cards can be used to optimal effect. The rite begins and ends in silence, like the silence that framed existence before the Marassa began their childlike play.

The materials you will need are cornmeal, a plate of food, a glass of water, a cup of water, a bowl of water, incense, a red candle, and a bit of earth; the Marassa card (No. VI), the Legba card (Rada 6), Les Morts card (No. XIII), and the Four Aces. It is best to do this rite while standing on the Earth. Sacrifices offered to the Dead and libations are always poured onto the Earth. If this Earth connection is not possible during the rite, collect the liquids and foods and later place them upon the Earth.

MARASSA

Enter the space of the ritual both physically and mentally. Concentrate on the Marassa. Allow who they are to move through you like the wind. The more that you know of the Marassa, the more frequently you call them to you, the easier it will become. Find or invent a litany of their praise names. Such a litany for the sun is given on page 79. It is a complex model. Keep the litany very simple so that it does not distract from your concentration.

Move from concentration to trance. Concentration is an intense intellectual attention, and trance is concentration with the addition of a strong emotional current. Begin softly singing the litany below your breath. Repeat it over and over, faster then slower, faster then slower. This is a great assist in moving to a trance state.

Imagine your hands as very young. Make the sign of the Marassa with both of your hands. The sign consists of spreading the small finger and the thumb as far apart as possible while bending the three middle fingers toward the palm of the hand. The thumb and small finger represent the Marassa. Next, bring the thumb and the small finger together while slowly unfolding the three middle fingers. The union of the Marassa is seen in the touching of the thumb and small finger. This is the completion of the gesture. The three middle fingers affirm the creation and existence of a third element, which is the relation of the Twins one to another.

Use the thumb and small finger of each hand to simultaneously draw the mirror elements of the Marassa vèvè with cornmeal. Dipping both of your hands simultaneously into the bowl of water, create roads

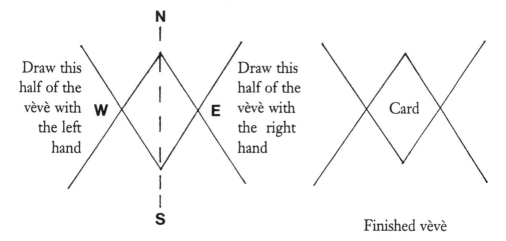

Draw this half of the vèvè with the left hand

Draw this half of the vèvè with the right hand

Card

Finished vèvè

of water moving inward from the north and the south and touching the vèvè. Then do the same from the east and the west. Let your singing chant become very intense, and climax at a high point of intensity by placing the Marassa card in the center of the vèvè. Note that in this and the following rituals it is *never* necessary to wet the cards. The water touches the cornmeal, not the cards.

With the calling of the Marassa, the practitioner has constructed a usable magickal universe. With the Marassa all is possible. Through them, we and the loa immediately spring into being.

We have brought into being the elements of the play. To create a web, a means of communication between those elements is the domain of Legba and his tool is the crossroads.

LEGBA OF THE CROSSROADS

Concentrate on Legba. Move into active trance through a singing chant as described in the Marassa section.

Imagine your hands as very old. Using your dominant hand, take a pinch of cornmeal and bring it to your mouth. Breathe through your mouth onto the cornmeal. Legba is the messenger of the loa, the opener of the way, the carrier of the word. Air or breath is the medium of the word.

With cornmeal, draw the vèvè of Legba over the vèvè and card of the Marassa.

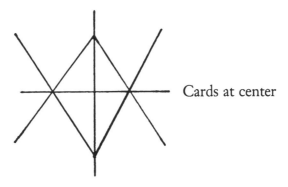

Cards at center

Again, create the roads of water. Place the Rada Legba card over the Marassa card while releasing all the power you have amassed.

Our universe has been created and a connecting webbing has been forged between its elements; we are now ready to offer Sacrifice.

THE DEAD/THE ANCESTORS

We are part of an unbroken chain which is composed of our family ancestors and, in a more inclusive sense, all members of the human family from all times. This chain reaches from the most distant past into the unimaginable future. As are all chains, this chain is only as strong as its weakest link. Sacrifices in the form of food and drink and the entertainment provided by an enthusiastically told story serve to fortify those family spirits which form the links of this chain.

The dead or the ancestors are those who have left the Visible World and journeyed into the World of the Invisibles. As the Angel of Death says in *Our Name is Melancholy* (Wendell, 1992, p. 307), "I am the point of contact between your world and eternity." It is from this eternity that the dead offer their help. The reciprocity inherent in the relationship of family is not severed by death's touch.

The purpose of this section of the rite is to feed the ancestors and to call on their support in all of life's activities.

Lift the plate containing the food with both hands. Make the crossroads figure in the air. After it is complete, kiss the plate and pass it through the center of the crossroads (drawn in the air); briefly release the plate with a tossing motion. Say words to this effect:

> *To all those whose names are remembered.*
> *To all those whose Names are forgotten.*
> *I give you to eat.*
> *To all those who have come before.*
> *To all those who will come after.*
> *I offer sustenance.*
>
> **—Martinié, 1986, p. 23**

Continue to hold the plate through the center of the crossroads and allow at least one bit of remembering to come into your thoughts. This could consist of a name, an incident, or a tale. If the information is not consciously recognizable, it may originate from the future or long ago in the past. Pay particular attention to names or information that are repeated a number of times. This might indicate a special type of communication.

Set the plate down in the top right quarter of the vèvè and repeat the preceding actions and words using the cup, substituting "drink" for "eat."

Place the cup in the top left quarter of the vèvè. Pick up the Ancestors or Les Morts card. Tell the spirits represented by the card about the rite you are performing. Make the telling into a tale. Good, animated stories are always more appreciated than a dry recitation of events. Ask these dead for their assistance. Place the card over the Rada Legba card.

At this point, a ritual space has been constructed, connections made between its elements, and the dead and the ancestors honored. The time is right for contact with the Mysteries.

THE MYSTERIES

To prepare for your contact with the Mysteries, you will need the following:

> FIRE: a red candle to the La Flambeau mysteries
> WATER: a bowl filled with water for the Congo Mysteries
> AIR: incense for the Rada Mysteries
> EARTH: actual soil for the Santería energies
> The four aces, attributed to Kether

Place the four cards of Kether at the cardinal points around the vèvè: Damballah La Flambeau to the south, in the station of elemental Fire; Ayida Wedo in the west, in the station of elemental Water;

Damballah Wedo in the east, in the station of elemental Air; Olodumare to the north, in the station of elemental Earth.

Take the candle, light it, pass it through the crossroads, and position it on the card of Damballah La Flambeau. Perform a singing chant to Damballah La Flambeau.

Take the glass filled with water, pass it through the crossroads, and position it on the card of Ayida Wedo. Perform a singing chant to Ayida Wedo.

Take the incense, light it, pass it through the crossroads, and place it on the card of Damballah Wedo. Perform a singing chant to Damballah Wedo.

Take the earth, pass it through the crossroads, and place it on the card of Olodumare. Perform a singing chant to Olodumare.

Draw the Water Road to the four cards as before while chanting to Legba to open the Door to the Mysteries, and to the Dead that they may pass into your life and offer their assistance.

The basic rite to honor and call the Marassa, Legba, the Ancestors/the Dead, and the Mysteries is now complete.

The performance of this rite provides for the accumulation of

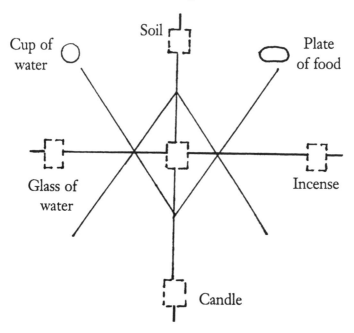

Soil

Cup of water

Plate of food

Glass of water

Incense

Candle

power or grace and opens the way for the spirits of Voodoo. This rite can be performed anytime; it is best to perform it often.

RITUAL OF SACRIFICE

TO ANCESTORS

If the cards indicate a sacrifice to the Ancestors would be beneficial, the following practices may be used. The general ritual form can follow the Ancestor/Dead rite on page 222. No vèvè is necessary.

Remembered Ancestor

Use the person's name and use food and drink that they preferred in life. Say prayers from the religion they belonged to during their life. The term "offerings" is better used in describing what is given to known ancestors. If the personality is remembered, they have perhaps taken only the first steps to becoming loa. "Sacrifice" is used more properly in speaking of foods and things given to the loa.

Forgotten Ancestor

Use any information you know of the person. Their country of origin, a country to which they moved. Use general foods and drinks you believe they would have eaten in life.

General Ancestor Rite

Use a phrase such as "all those who have gone before me." Fresh water and food prepared from a grain are good sacrifices.

TO THE LOA AND ORISHA

If sacrifice to a loa or orisha is indicated by the cards, an acceptable food or object may be found on pages 11–17. Next find the vèvè of the loa or ritual drawing of the orisha on the page that describes that spirit. Construct the vèvè or drawing using cornmeal and place the sacrifice in the center of the drawing. Trace the Water Roads from north and south, east and west, into the drawing while chanting the name of the spirit and inviting the spirit to partake of the sacrifice. If food has been used and left at the crossroads or at an altar, its desiccation without mold is a sure sign that the spirit has taken the sacrifice; however, the presence of mold by no means indicates that the sacrifice has been rejected.

BIRTHING THE DECK

Under your care, the deck has the potential to become a living organism. It can incarnate a unique individual spirit that is a combination of your essence and that of the deck itself. This rite is meant to assist this spirit in coming into being.

Take some of your hair and nail clippings and place them on the deck. Wrap the deck and these items in a white cloth. Leave the package in a dark place for nine days. On the ninth day, bring the deck out into the light and perform a rite in which you name the deck. Use whatever rite or process of naming was used to give you your own name. Write the name you give the deck on a piece of paper. Celebrate the birth and naming of the deck by offering money to the poor to buy food and by preparing a meal for yourself and the deck. Offer the deck small portions of the foods and liquids used in the meal by placing them before the deck.

Gather together the hair, nail clippings, paper on which the name was written, and the residue of the food and liquids fed to the deck. Sprinkle the food with the liquids. Give the majority of the food and liquids back to the Earth. Keep a small portion of the damp food.

Place these items in a clay jar with a lid and keep the jar in a safe place. If the cards are lost or destroyed, the contents of this jar can be used to reconstruct the spirit of the deck through the redoing of the initial rite using the materials within the jar.

If you decide to stop using the deck, take the jar and deck into the woods. Break the jar at the foot of a tree and hang the deck lightly wrapped in a black cloth from one of the branches.

CIRCLE OF CARDS

After birthing the deck, this practice can be used to explore attraction to the spirits of the various cards.

Lay the cards out in a large rough circle with each card close but not touching its partners. Sit within the center of the circle of cards and repeat the name you have given the deck over and over, varying the speed of the repetition. Stop when you sense that you have focused your self upon the name. Without looking at the cards, move around the circle, feeling with the palms of your hands for subtle differences between the cards. This can be done by holding the palms over the cards or by actually touching and holding the cards. Are some cards hotter or cooler than others? Do some feel attractive and some repellent? Keep a record of your findings and see if any card repeats a particular sensation.

When you have finished, thank the deck and gather up the cards.

SPIRITUAL AFFINITY: DRESSING THE DECK

It is a good idea to keep the deck dressed in a cloth. The color of the cloth you choose determines what spiritual influences you wish to enter the deck. Keep the deck in a white cloth if you wish to isolate it from its surroundings; this isolation is a type of ritual purity. Keep it in a black cloth if you want it to absord the energies of its surroundings. If you have an affinity with the La Flambeau nation, keep the deck in a red cloth. If your affinity is with the Congo nation, use a blue cloth. An affinity with the Rada nation calls for a gold cloth; with Santería, cloth of a rich brown fabric.

The clothing of the deck can change in much the same manner as you change your clothing. For example, if the deck is normally dressed in a black cloth and kept in an area dedicated to specific spiritual forces, when you take it outside it may be a good idea to dress the deck in white for the trip. This would tend to preserve those forces called into the deck by its normal surroundings.

TO HEAT UP THE DECK

In Voodoo, activities or rituals that are said to "heat up" are used to bring power into objects or the participants. The purpose of the following two rites is to heat up or bring power into the cards so that the readings will carry more spirit, be more accurate, and be more easily understood.

First take the deck, rub your palms together, and let the heat radiate into the deck. This is feeding a part of yourself to the deck, creating a link. Lift the deck and breathe warm air between the cards. This is warming and creates a stronger link between the reader and the deck. Hold the deck before you and whisper that it is time for the spirits of the deck to attend. Chant the verse from the card of Legba:

> Odu Legba, Papa Legba,
> Open the door
> Your children await.
>
> Papa Legba, open the door,
> Your children await.

Then take the deck as a whole and pass it through a crossroads inscribed in the air (see The Dead/The Ancestors, p. 222). The deck moves into the land of the spirits as it is tossed through the crossroads. Take one card from the deck and rub it between your hands; let it absorb the oils your hands produce. Without looking at the title of the card, insert it into the deck again. Tell it to share what it has received with the other cards.

Either of the rites described above can be performed before every reading or on some regular basis. This will ensure the attention of the loa during your card readings.

SELF AS CROSSROAD:
THE ANCIENT BALANCE

This practice can be used to strengthen the practitioner's contact with the spirit of a chosen card. In this rite, the body itself is used as a crossroads.

Darken the room in which you are working. Place the chosen card in front of a mirror. Place a candle nearby and seat yourself so that the image of the card can be clearly seen in the mirror and you can touch both the card and its image. Concentrate on the actual card and then upon the image of the card in the mirror. Notice the differences and similarities. Rub the palms of your hands together. Reach out, holding your right palm over the actual card and your left palm over the mirror reflection. Absorb both cards into the palms of your hands and move the sensation of this absorption through your arms, through your chest, and then into your head. This action can be repeated several times.

A RITUAL TO BRING
BLESSING

Obtain something personal from the subject of the reading. The subject of the reading could be another person or it could be yourself. While concentrating on the object you have acquired, consciously lay out a favorable reading. Place the cards around or on top of the object in such a manner as to indicate a favorable outcome. Leave the reading to "cook," that is, to completely mingle the forces called by the reading with the object. The Blessing will pass onto the recipient you appointed.

TO AFFECT THE OUTCOME
OF AN EVENT

First, decide whether you actually know enough of the possible consequences of the event to exercise this kind of control. Next ask yourself if you have the personal power and relationship with the loa necessary to engage in the working. If the answers to both questions are yes, then either of the following two practices will prove effective.

1. Concentrate on the outcome you wish to occur. Consciously choose cards to represent that particular outcome and lay them out as a reading. Offer sacrifice to Legba and the Mysteries represented by the cards each day over a three-day period.

2. Perform a reading while concentrating on the event and its desired outcome. Examine the reading for cards carrying forces you do not wish to be present. Offer sacrifice to the spirits represented by those cards, asking them to leave. Consciously pick desired cards and lay them over the unwanted cards. Offer sacrifice to Legba and the Mysteries represented by the desired cards each day over a three-day period.

READINGS

While the New Orleans Voodoo Tarot is mainly designed to assist the user in developing a closer relationship with the loa and the orisha, it can be effectively used as a tool for practical divination. The following spreads for readings can be used in either a practical or esoteric manner. The difference lies in the *type* of question posed in the card reading. The practitioner may ask practical or esoteric questions of the cards. For example, the *Legba's Cane* spread can be used to discern elements necessary to "open up" a situation. The situation may consist of finding a lover for a friend or identifying those elements necessary to call a stronger Ogoun force into the temple during ritual. One caution: word your queries as precisely as possible. The spirits which oversee divination usually have a pronounced element of the Trickster.

In order to facilitate a more complete relationship with the loa, the Contemplation that follows the description of each card will usually be of more importance than the Divination. A general approach would be to use the divinatory meaning of the cards to secure your stability in the world, to obtain those resources necessary to live. Use the Contemplation to develop a stronger relationship with the spirits.

One of the unique aspects of the Voodoo Tarot is the recommendation of a sacrifice by certain card readings. See pages 11–17 for a list of cards and appropriate sacrifices. The ritual section describes a good method for offering these sacrifices.

The vèvès shown in the readings can be visualized on the surface where the cards are laid out or they can be drawn with cornmeal. It is usually preferable to do the latter. If you do not use cornmeal, it is possible to simply trace the figure with your hands. A technique I have found effective in the actual drawing of the figures is to use both hands to simultaneously draw symmetrical portions of the vèvès.

Lay the cards on top of the cornmeal as shown in the readings. After the reading is complete, gather up the cards and disperse the vèvè using both hands. Breaking the pattern of the vèvè releases the power it holds. You can absorb the power by eating a bit of the cornmeal or pressing a bit to your forehead or the back of your neck. Using the back of the neck invites a deep in-dwelling by the loa. Leave the used cornmeal at a crossroads or scatter it upon the Earth.

A possession of the hands is very useful in these readings. This is a type of partial possession in which a loa is invited to enter the reader's hands and choose the cards. An effective way to bring on this type of possession is to draw the vèvè, rub your hands together briskly, and position them over the drawing. You will feel heat radiating out of your hands and into the vèvè. This feeds and calls the loa of the vèvè. After a few seconds you will notice an influx of power into your outstretched hands. Allow the power in the hands to build; it is a pleasant sensation. Use this power in the hands to choose the cards. Flick your hands downward, preferably over the Earth, to disperse this power. It takes some practice to be able to hold the possession long enough for the reading. The rubbing technique can be repeated several times during the course of the reading.

It is best to work directly on the ground, but an excellent substitute is a mirror lying flat on a table. The vèvès can be drawn on this mirror and then the cards laid upon it. I like to use a mirror with a deep blue tint.

This deck is new, and the use of vèvès in the readings is a new technique. The readings here use eight vèvès, representing loa of the twenty-two road cards, that are well suited to shed light on specific questions or situations. There are also readings using traditional Tarot layouts, the Celtic Cross, and the Tree of Life.

Both the cards and the vèvès call upon spirits using the means of the visual arts. The combination of visual elements, card and vèvè, creates a strong artistic impact pleasing to both spirit and practitioner. This is an excellent combination for experimentation with other vèvès or loa you feel close to. You can apply the basic hand techniques to other vèvès given in this book and request that the loa of the vèvè provide you with a scheme for reading the cards, using the points of its vèvè.

SACRIFICE

Purpose: To tell if a sacrifice is needed and if so, to whom.

Three pennies are needed for this reading. Calling on Legba with a singing litany, draw a vèvè in the manner described on page 231, drop the coins onto the center of the crossroads. If the majority fall to the Cane side, a sacrifice is needed. If the majority fall to the opposite side, sacrifice is unnecessary.

A card placed in the middle of the crossroads will indicate the spirit or process that will bestow benefit if sacrifice is offered.

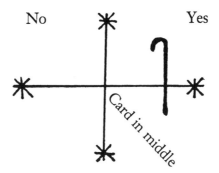

LEGBA'S CANE

Purpose: To obtain the key to opening the door of a situation. Knowledge of the means to overcome obstacles.

Legba uses the cane pictured in this vèvè to power his movements. Card 1 placed here shows the way to opening the door and moving through it. Card 2, placed opposite the cane, closes the door and serves to block the way. The proper sacrifices can ease or strengthen the situation.

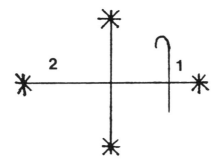

CROSSROADS

Purpose: To examine a situation from the viewpoint of past, present, and future influences. Influences from the Visible and Invisible Worlds.

Cards: 1: Future influences (East)

2: Present influences (Middle)

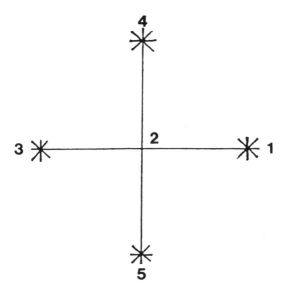

3: Past influences (West)

4: Influences from the Visible World (Top)

5: Influences from the Invisible World (Bottom)

All of these influences can be strengthened or weakened through sacrifice.

MARASSA

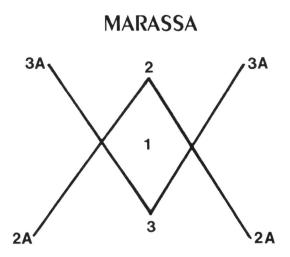

Purpose: This spread of the cards can be used to look for deep sources of spiritual power or to get to the root of a practical situation.

Cards: 1: The Middle card is the root or source card.

2 and 3: These cards point to the two primary influences that support the root card. Card 2 shows influences from the Visible World on the root card and card 3 shows influences from the Invisible World on the root card. If the root card describes a desirable situation, you may want to strengthen the influences represented by those cards through sacrifice. If the root card describes an undesirable situation, you may want to sacrifice to sweeten or placate the influences. The sacrifice is the same in both cases. It is your intention or request that differs.

2A and 3A: These cards serve to more clearly define the influences shown by cards 2 and 3.

ERZULIE

Purpose: To estimate the influences on an affair of love or union.

Cards: 1: The state of the affair. A card laid over and crossing this or any other cards would describe hostile influences.

      2: Past influences (West)

      3: Future influences (East)

      4: Influences from the Visible World

      5: Influences from the Invisible World

If this reading moves in undesired ways, a general sacrifice to Erzulie may be in order.

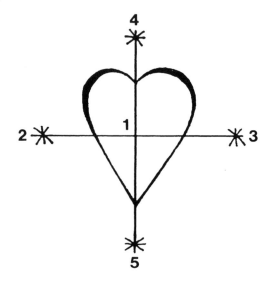

THE DEAD

Purpose: To discover effect of the Dead on a situation.

Cards: 1: The effect of one or more of the known dead.

      2: The effect of one or more of the unknown dead.

Sacrifice is very important here and in the Ancestors reading on page 238. The Dead or the Ancestors depend on us as we do on them.

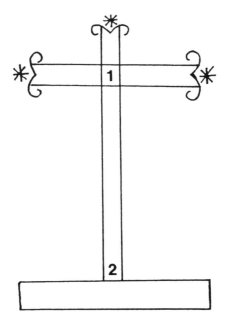

We share a symbiotic relationship. As the Dead fare, so we fare. If we reach to the heights, we do so upon their shoulders.

TI BON ANGE AND GROS BON ANGE

Purpose: To trace deep influences on one's individual will and the ability to open up to universal love and grace.

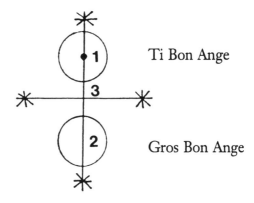

Cards: 1: Influences of the individual will of the questioner.

2: Influences on the ability of the questioner to partake in the grace of universal love.

3: The relationship of individual will to the universal flow of grace.

Card 3 is pivotal; a weak connection here can be strengthened by taking action, including sacrifice.

ANCESTORS

Purpose: To judge the effect ancestors have upon a situation. Ancestors in this case are members of your close biological family, both living and dead.

Cards: 1, Head card: the influence of living ancestors.

2, Body card: the effect of remembered dead ancestors.

3, Tail card: the effect of forgotten dead ancestors.

The use of sacrifice is of particular importance in this and the Dead reading.

THE CELTIC CROSS: A BRIDGE

The Celtic Cross is a traditional reading that is often used with standard Tarot decks. The reading is included in this section to serve

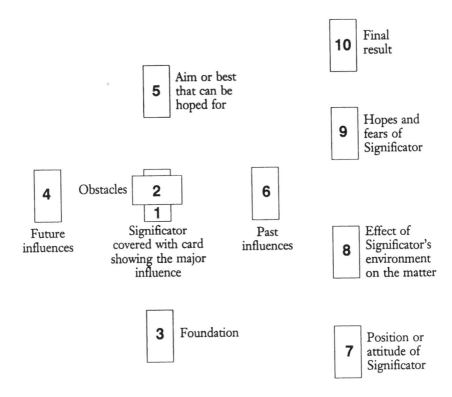

as a bridge connecting the reader's present knowledge of Tarot to the cards of the New Orleans Voodoo Tarot.

Owen Knight, a modern bard and keeper of the ancient Celtic religious traditions, often stresses in his conversations that the religious pantheon of the Celts welcomed with open arms the gods and goddesses of those people with whom the Celts came into contact. The newly encountered Deities were incorporated into the Celtic liturgy. The houngan or mambo of Voodoo and the druid of the Celtic religions stand together in this openhanded attitude toward other Deities and religious practices.

The diagram of the Celtic Cross draws upon Waite's (1971, p. 299) description of this reading. The Significator card is consciously chosen from the deck and represents the person or object of the reading. The Significator card is covered with a card showing the major influence on the matter.

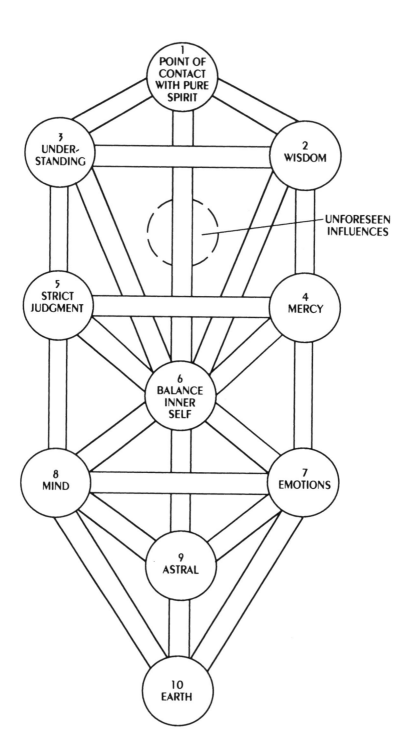

TREE OF LIFE

Purpose: To define in detail the influences on an important life situation. This reading is never done lightly.

Cards: Select one for each of the ten vessels and one for the eleventh, which represents unforeseen influences. (A large surface is needed for this layout.) The vessels describe an aspect of the situation as noted in the diagram. The cards that you have selected show influences on these aspects of the situation. To identify adverse influences to the original cards, pick a new card and place it across the card now occupying the vessel. This new card shows influences that block or cross the original card. If the original card describes a preferred influence, you would want to avoid or placate the forces behind the blocking card through sacrifice. If the original card describes an unwanted influence, you would sacrifice to strengthen the block.

DIVINATORY MEANINGS
OF THE CARDS

This section is provided for quick reference during readings.

THE TWENTY-TWO ROADS

0 Damballah and Ayida's World Egg (The Fool/Aleph)
Divination: Surprise; the unexpected; beginnings; influence from the Highest in spiritual matters; possible disruption of physical matters.

I Dr. John (The Magus/Beth)
Divination: Craft; consummate skill in the matter at hand; occult powers or wisdom; ability to see root causes clearly; identification of the individual Will with a greater or more inclusive Will.

II Marie Laveau (High Priestess/Gimel)
Divination: Connection is possible between seemingly diverse elements. The words of Aleister Crowley speak most elegantly of Our Lady: "Pure, exalted and gracious influence enters the matter. Hence change, alteration, increase and decrease, fluctuation" (Book of Thoth).

III Ayizan (The Empress/Daleth)
Divination: Love, beauty, pleasure, and success. Protection for women's affairs and the just in general. Concern for purity of devotion.

IV Loco (The Emperor/Tzaddi)

Divination: Protection, ambition, victory, strife, conquest, war.

V Master of the Head (The Heirophant/Vav)

Divination: Realization of purpose, initiation, teachings, assistance from forces perceived as highly placed.

VI Marassa (Lovers/Zayin)

Divination: Acceptance of differences. The possibility of turning a perceived threat to your benefit by emphasizing common ground or interests. Childlike qualities; childish fear, anger, or mirth.

VII Dance (The Chariot/Cheth)

Divination: Transcendence of a situation through ecstatic physical action. Triumph, victory, constructive or destructive adherence to set forms of action.

VIII (or XI) Possession (Strength or Lust/Teth)

Divination: Strength; a bursting free from the bounds of limiting belief; courage and the sufficient energy to act effectively.

IX Couché (The Hermit/Yod)

Divination: Retreat from daily life for a spiritual purpose, internal inspiration, realization of the amount others sacrifice that we may grow and prosper; a sense of the sacredness of all life.

X The Market (The Wheel/Kaph)

Divination: A realization upon which your works or very existence depends; a rapid change of fortune.

XI (or VIII) Secret Societies (Justice/Adjustment/Lamed)

Divination: The moment when all hangs in the balance; cases of law, cases of conscience, pangs of conscience calling one to action; recourse to the Ancestors for a decision in the matter at hand.

XII Zombi (Hanged Man/Mem)

Divination: Sacrifice externally motivated and enforced. Questions of will and the questioning of will cause resolve to decay and failure of the spirit and/or body.

XIII Les Morts (Death/Nun)
Divination: Change, flux. Messages from the dead, in particular from the querier's ancestors. Probable need to make offerings to the ancestors.

XIV Ti Bon Ange (Temperance or Art/Samekh)
Divination: A call to action based on who you are and your place in the world; assertion of self; discovery of the True Self; an overcoming of obstacles to the expression of the True Self.

XV Courir Le Mardi Gras (The Devil/Ayin)
Divination: Uncontrolled energies; material considerations pushed to their limits; creativity exercised regardless of effect; questions of individuality and interdependence.

XVI Deluge (Blasted Tower/Pe)
Divination: Sacrifice, unavoidable and often misunderstood; violent physical or emotional upheaval revealing core issues or aspects of the self.

XVII Z'Étoile (The Star/Hé)
Divination: Coming to terms with one's fate and obtaining the clear sight and strength this action brings, dedication to a lifework. The road is clear, the Star in sight.

XVIII Magick Mirror (The Moon/Qoph)
Divination: Magick and sorcery, occult power, deception.

XIX Gros Bon Ange (The Sun/Resh)
Divination: Influx or helpful energy; success possibly earned by effort or possibly not. Love freely given without regard to object; happiness, joy. Universal rather than particular love.

XX Ancestors (Last Judgment or Aeon/Shin)
Divination: Final judgment, an understanding of the worth and meaning of one's actions within the context of the procession of life.

XXI Carnival (The World/Tau)

Divination: Points to a greater appreciation of the elements of the question or concern that is addressed in the reading. Physical aspects of the question or concern; release from a problem through physical means.

Wild Card: Les Barons (Joker)

Divination: Extreme unexpected turn of events; a sense of humor pulls one through dire circumstances.

PETRO (WANDS/FIRE)

Damballah La Flambeau (Ace of Wands)

Divination: Natural force, strength, and energy are available for use. If the reading indicates opposition by this card, the questioner may expect to meet with strong antagonism.

Nan Nan Bouclou La Flambeau (Two of Wands)

Divination: Influence; individual will focused in such a way as to bring change upon another, for good or ill.

Guedeh La Flambeau (Three of Wands)

Divination: Power, strength, magnetism, all generally—though not necessarily—of a sexual nature. Possible tendency toward arrogance.

Agwé La Flambeau (Four of Wands)

Divination: Union of opposites, which may express itself as a marriage; the quiet before the storm; the unexpected (as in fire and water giving rise to air); shifting emotions; unexpected shifts, safe haven constructed with much labor.

Ogoun La Flambeau (Five of Wands)

Divination: Pain, especially physical; an aching questioning of one's actions leading to despair. War. Strife, internal or external. Actions against life and death must lead to regret. (Constructive use of a potentially destructive force. The ability to still question things and ideas to which one has given much.)

Legba La Flambeau (Six of Wands)
Divination: Victory, obstacles swept aside, the first necessary victories of the Pure Fool. A newly initiated elder flexes his or her first powers. "There is no grace, there is no guilt, do what thou wilt."

Erzulie La Flambeau (Seven of Wands)
Divination: Forceful and decisive action in the matter at hand, bringing to bear the full force of emotional involvement in the situation; swift emotional ordeals leading to a refinement of personality or spiritual essence; rage; persons united by anger.

Simbi La Flambeau (Eight of Wands)
Divination: Short-lived perfection; an uncovering of hidden motives or aspects of the affair at hand; secrecy with a tendency toward stubbornness; plots. Rapid thought or action.

Masa La Flambeau (Nine of Wands)
Divination: Strong emotion bubbles under a calm surface. Hidden passion; rapid, unpredictable change; strength through balance.

Azaka La Flambeau (Ten of Wands)
Divination: Oppression, cruelty. Hope based on the ability to imagine a better situation.

Petro Houngan (King/Knight of Wands)
The character traits associated with this card include fierceness, pride, and impulsiveness.

Physically such a person is likely to be a man with blond, red, or reddish-black hair and blue, hazel, or light-brown eyes.

Petro Mambo (Queen of Wands)
The individual described by this card exhibits authority, a magnetic kind of attraction; she is generous in friendship and love, where she is apt to take the lead.

Physically this woman may have red, gold, or reddish-black hair, and blue or brown eyes.

Petro La Place (Prince of Wands)
Personality traits of this card include nobility, strength, swiftness, and fairness of judgment.

Physically the object of this card is apt to be a young man with yellow or brownish-black hair and blue or gray eyes.

Petro Hounsis (Princess of Wands)
Character traits associated with this card include all intense states such as anger, love, ambition, enthusiasm, and vengeance. Her emotions are prone to rapid change.

Physically she is apt to be a young woman with gold or red hair and blue or light brown eyes.

CONGO (CUPS/WATER)

Ayida Wedo (Ace of Cups)
Divination: This card points to pleasure and happiness. The influence is that of the Great Mother, who creates freely through the subtle pressure of the Waters.

Gran Ibo (Two of Cups)
Divination: Harmony born of a deep and abiding wisdom. A marriage in the Visible or Invisible World as an expression of harmony, plenty.

Manman Brigitte (Three of Cups)
Divination: Correct judgment; full measure of all good things upon proper understanding of the situation at hand; a verdict of law that offers benefit, pleasure, and prosperity; the understanding of death gives one access to the pleasures of life.

La Baleine (Four of Cups)
Divination: The gentle care of the mother; a desire to return to safe

haven; a desire to nurture; overprotectiveness imposing unnecessary limits.

Ogoun Bhalin'dio (Five of Cups)
Divination: Trouble; worry; loss; possible onset of disease. (Recourse to or ability to act as Healer.)

Shi-Li-Bo Nouvavou and Dan-i (Six of Cups)
Divination: The joy of will manifest, the questioner's Work in its fullness.

La Sirène (Seven of Cups)
Divination: In affairs of the emotions there is to be a bridging or a joining of elements. A marriage is the most obvious manifestation whether the elements of the marriage are two people or a bringing together of ways in which the world is being perceived. The "siren song" of deception, causing one to forget his or her will.

Simbi d'l'eau (Eight of Cups)
Divination: Correct impulse leading to equivocal action; a sense of the matter at hand which cannot be put into words; a breakdown of communication; falsehood through confusion, not malice. The sense of a confusing situation mishandled through lack of interpretative effort.

Madame La Lune (Nine of Cups)
Divination: Cyclic change, a return to beginnings after a cycle is complete, orderly change. Enchantment, happiness.

Gran Bois (Ten of Cups)
Divination: Favorable outcome when the last words are said and the last things done.

Congo Hougan (King/Knight of Cups)
The character of the person aspected by this card is generally passive and given to the imaginative imagery used in poetry. He can be enthusiastic, but the enthusiasm easily falls away. He can be very idealistic.

Physically this person is inclined to have light brown to blond or brownish-black hair and blue or light brown eyes.

Congo Mambo (Queen of Cups)
She has a dreamy and tranquil personality, which tends to express itself poetically.

Physically she is likely to be a woman with black or brown hair with a golden hue and brown or blue eyes.

Congo La Place (Prince of Cups)
Characteristics of the personality described by this card are a calm surface covering a fiery interior, subtlety, secret violence, and craft.

Physically this card describes a young man with brown or brownish-black hair and gray or brown eyes.

Congo Hounsis (Princess of Cups)
The character of the person identified with this card is dreamy and sweet. She is the great romantic.

Physically she is a young woman with brown or black hair and blue or brown eyes.

RADA (SWORDS/AIR)

Damballah Wedo (Ace of Swords)
Divination: Great energy called to do good or ill. Stationary forces are roused and called into action.

Nan Nan Bouclou (Two of Swords)
Divination: Mutual benefit based upon the experience of and devotion to the Grand Mother.

Guedeh (Three of Swords)
Divination: Sorrow of a deep and brooding nature; the joy and gaiety that attends the release from this sorrow.

Agwé (Four of Swords)
Divination: Quiet in the presence of real or implied threat; trust that matters will turn out for the best.

Ogoun Ferraille (Five of Swords)
Divination: Loss, defeat, unfavorable outcome. (Bravery in the face of certain loss.)

Legba (Six of Swords)
Divination: A task that may be accomplished through words. The door opens; obstacles are removed.

Erzulie Freda Dahomey (Seven of Swords)
Divination: Imaginings beyond possibility, the jolt of shattered dreams.

Simbi (Eight of Swords)
Divination: Magick used. Possible overapplication of force for, in contrast, a petty end. Complex means used when more simple would suffice. Unstable result (effects gained through magick tend to lack temporal persistence).

Masa (Nine of Swords)
Divination: A move, such as change in residence, or the intercession of a courier. An expected gift arrives, for good or ill.

Azaka (Ten of Swords)
Divination: Succumbing before the onslaught of inevitable forces, perseverance against great odds. Success at great price.

Rada Houngan (King/Knight of Swords)
Character traits of individuals covered by this card include courage, swiftness, and readiness to attack.

Physically the individual is likely to have dark brown or black hair and dark eyes.

Rada Mambo (Queen of Swords)
The character of the woman aspected by this card shows the traits of

individuality, keen observation, subtlety, and accuracy of perception. She is graceful and loves dancing and any physical activity that involves balancing.

Physically this woman is likely to have grayish hair and light brown eyes.

Rada La Place (Prince of Swords)
The persons described by this card are brilliant in argument and intellectual discussion but lack conviction. The points they make so well are unrelated, one contradicting the other.

Physically this person is apt to be a young man with dark hair and dark eyes.

Rada Hounsis (Princesses of Swords)
Character traits of individuals covered by this card include wisdom in the handling of material affairs, ability to translate dreams into physical reality, firmness, and aggressiveness.

Physically she is apt to be a young woman with light brown or brownish-black hair and light brown or blue eyes.

SANTERÍA (DISKS OR PENTACLES/EARTH)

Olodumare (Ace of Disks)
Divination: The root sense of materiality. The presence of all material possibilities; from soaring wealth to crushing poverty.

Olofi (Two of Disks)
Divination: Change, especially that change that brings stability to a situation or relationship.

Oyá (Three of Disks)
Divination: An abrupt change in a situation; gain in the marketplace; turn for the better in matters of business.

Obatalá (Four of Disks)

Divination: Wisdom displayed in the matter at hand; fair judgment; correct assessment of a situation; mastery of a situation through calm, deliberate action; presents given as tokens of respect.

Oggún (Five of Disks)

Divination: Containment of great internal or external pressures; stress; strain; worry that arises as a result of this constant pressure. (The strength to stand solidly before threat or adversity.)

Elegguá (Six of Disks)

Divination: Proper care in the matter at hand ensures favorable outcome, the influence of a child or childlike person.

Oshún (Seven of Disks)

Divination: Emotions manifest in concrete fashion; a sacrament can be defined as an outward sign of an invisible or interior state. The creation of a sacrament which will bring to fruition some emotional involvement. For example, the purchase of a house can be viewed as an outward sign of emotional involvement in a social or biological family. Possible disappointment in the solid forms love takes.

Shangó (Eight of Disks)

Divination: Family obligations fulfilled bring bounty to all; family obligations ignored bring destruction; wise rule; control of a situation used or misused. Excellent skill.

Yemayá (Nine of Disks)

Divination: Pregnant with idea or child; abundance; gain; a bequest of parental bounty.

Ochosi (Ten of Disks)

Divination: Accumulation; that which was gathered spoils if not put to use.

Santero (King/Knight of Disks)

Character traits of individuals covered by this card include a strong sense of the holiness of the earth, which leads to patience and industry in physical matters (these traits differ from those described in the Thoth or Golden Dawn Tarot).

Physically, this man is liable to have dark hair and dark eyes.

Santera (Queen of Disks)
The personality of such a woman is characterized by affection and a large capacity for the giving and receiving of love. Dire are the consequences if her love and loyalty are betrayed.

Physically she is likely to be a woman with dark hair and dark eyes.

Oriaté (Prince of Disks)
The person associated with this card is apt to have a character that is competent, trustworthy, and reliable. He makes a good worker or manager.

Physically the person described by this card is likely to be a young man with dark brown or black hair and dark eyes.

Yaguó (Princesses of Disks)
Character traits associated with this card include benevolence, strength, beauty, and fearless protection.

Physically she is a young woman with blue-black, rich brown, or red-brown hair and dark eyes.

THE LAST JUDGMENT:
AN AFTERWORD

All begins and ends with the loa. As this book was written life flowed around and through me. It took and it gave. There was birth, death, and rebirth into the land of the spirits. Perhaps all that we can hold onto are those moments of life that impart the spark of eternity. Those moments of life that communicate the mystery of existence.

The mind loves to create criteria and to judge. This work will be judged by many, using various criteria. Taking the prerogative of author, my mind has already judged. If this book brings the reader in any way closer to the mystery that is life, it will have succeeded. It will have been worthy of the sacrifice of trees and other resources used in its printing. This is the relevant criterion for me. This is the thin line on which worth hangs.

APPENDIX:
CONTACTS & SUPPLIES

COME ON DOWN FOR THE MARDI GRAS

Any time that you come to New Orleans, the following stores, galleries, groups, and individuals can serve as an introduction to the metaphysical and occult community. While a number of the listings do not deal directly with Voodoo, they still give a sense of what it means to work with the spirits in New Orleans.

Alternatives: A New Age newspaper with much more substance than is usually found in the genre. Frequent articles by Leilah Wendell and Daniel Kemp. 5500 Prytania St., No. 335, New Orleans, LA 70115; phone (504) 865-8431.

Bahlasti Papers: The monthly publication of Kali Lodge, Ordo Templi Orientis in New Orleans. Literature and art meet head-on in this newsletter. Editorials which bring mysticism and Malkuth together are featured. Please see Kali Lodge.

Black Moon Publishing: Books and journals dealing with night-side magicks and spirituality. Editorial desk and archives in New Orleans. Send orders and inquiries to P.O. Box 19469, Cincinnati, OH 45219-0469.

Blue Bayou: Center for the state-chartered Religious Order of Witchcraft. Formerly the Witchcraft Shop, it was originally founded as an outlet for the selling of the tools of witchcraft and Voodoo. Shop, consultations. and card readings. 521 St. Philip St., New Orleans, LA 70116; phone (504) 522-7730.

Bottom of the Cup Tea Room: Books, jewelry, and gift items. Established in 1929. Psychics read in curtained cubicles located in the back of the stores. 616 Conti and 732 Royal, New Orleans, LA 70130; phone (504) 524-1997 or (504) 523-1204.

Divine Light: Occult books, oils, candles, and herbs. Private consultations. 3318 Magazine, New Orleans, LA 70115; phone (504) 899-6617.

Drumspeak: New Orleans–based drum group. Recordings of ritual drumming and instruction. Ace/Llewellyn Recordings, 1643 Lee Rd., Cleveland, OH 44118.

EOD (Esoteric Order of Dagon): Weavers of eclectic transcendental ritual with teleogenic and immortalist alchemy. Bill Seibert and Raven Graywalker. Contact c/o Black Moon Publishing (see Black Moon Publishing).

F & F Botanica: All manner of spiritual supplies with which to praise the spirit. More a celebration than a shop when Felix is present. 801 N. Broad St., New Orleans, LA 70119; phone (504) 482-9142.

Sallie Ann Glassman: Artist and ritualist. Her work is found on *The New Orleans Voodoo Tarot* and the *Enochian Tarot*. Signed original pastels of *The New Orleans Voodoo Tarot* cards are available for sale to collectors. A list of available works may be obtained from the artist: P.O. Box 15038, New Orleans, LA 70115.

Golden Leaves: Bookmart and metaphysical center. Psychic readings. charts, classes, lectures. 211 Phlox Ave., Metairie, LA 70001; phone (504) 888-5208.

Iraya Publications: Dedicated to bringing the darkness into focus. *The Book of Night* by Daniel Kemp, the most recent publication, is a book of short poetic glimpses into the "shining darkness." 5219 Magazine St., No. 2, New Orleans, LA 70115.

Jackson Square: Tarot and palm readings given by the readers who circle the square. Jackson Square Psychics Association is an organization which promotes licensed, ethical, and professional conduct and services. The French Quarter, in front of St. Louis Cathedral, New Orleans.

Ava Kay Jones: Voodoo and Yoruba priestess. Consultations, books, and supplies. This priestess is highly respected in the New Orleans Voodoo community. Phone (504) 866-3969.

Kali Lodge: A lodge of the Ordo Templi Orientis. This is a working lodge with a full schedule of Thelemic, Voodoo, and multisystem rites. Their marriage of Enochian and Voodoo in ritual is a heady brew. Publishers of *Bahlasti Papers*. P.O. Box 15038, New Orleans, LA 70115.

Marie Laveau's House of Voodoo: Books, religious and magical objects, readings, and consultations. The front room contains a beautiful and powerful Guedeh cross where offerings of coins may be left. A back room features a life-size display chronicling the movement of African-based spirituality from Africa to Haiti to New Orleans. 739 Bourbon St., New Orleans, LA 70130; phone (504) 581-3751.

Maison de la Lune Noire: Lodging for the esoteric traveler in the City of the Crescent Moon. 726 3rd St., New Orleans, LA 70130.

Muslima Moonpaki: Tours in French or English. A highly knowledgeable priestess whose work with snakes is particularly powerful. New Orleans; phone (504) 581-1111.

Mystic Curio: A curiosity shop featuring objects of interest from a variety of cultures. Many of the jewelry items and oils are made in the store. The owner is a wise man, well worth speaking to. 833 Royal St., New Orleans, LA 70116; phone (504) 581-7150.

Taboo Tattoo: Art for the skin of every description. If you see someone walking around with a vévé on the biceps, Taboo Tattoo probably did the work. P.O. Box 15038, New Orleans, LA 70115.

Voodoo Museum: The museum concentrates upon the historical aspects of Voodoo and emphasizes that Voodoo is a form of direct, earth-based spirituality. You are apt to find a combination of tourism and the real thing. A powerful painting of Marie Laveau by curator C. M. Gandalfo is on display in the gift shop. Various tours, consultations, readings, rituals, and blessings by paid admission. 724 Dumaine, New Orleans, LA 70116; phone (504) 523-7685.

Westgate Foundation: The foundation incorporates the following:
Westgate Press, publishers of books dedicated to the understanding of the essential nature of Azrael, the Angel of Death. *Our Name is Melancholy—The Complete Books of Azrael* by Leilah Wendel is the latest offering.
Westgate Museum/Gallery, focusing exclusively on art and literature dedicated to Azrael, the great Angle of Death. More commonly known as the "House of Death."
The Azrael Project Newsletter is also published by Westgate. It is the work of the foundation to reconcile Life with Death, rekindle primeval memory, and hopefully replace fear with love. The Museum/Gallery is one of New Orleans' most unique metaphysical attractions. Westgate, 5219 Magazine St., New Orleans, LA 70115; phone (504) 899-3077.

For consultations and ritual work I would highly recommend Oswan Chamani and Miriam Williams of The Voodoo Spiritual Temple, Courtney Willis of Technicians of the Sacred, or Rose Frank of Madre de Agua Temple.

The Voodoo Spiritual Temple is located at 716 N. Rampart, New

Orleans, LA 70116; phone (504) 522-9627. *The Times-Picayune* of New Orleans, a daily newspaper, has printed a number of favorable articles on Chamani and Williams.

Technicians of the Sacred may be reached at Suite 310, 1317 N. San Fernando Blvd., Burbank, CA 91504. This is also the contact for *Société Journal,* The International Religious and Magical Order of Société, La Couleuvre Noire, The Neo-African Network, and Ordo Templi Orientis Antigua. A very complete general religious and magical supply catalog is also available through this address.

Madre de Agua Temple is in the process of moving from the French Quarter and is making plans to open a soup kitchen for the poor in another section of New Orleans. Rose Frank and her work are the subject of an award-winning documentary film. Write me in care of Inner Traditions, the publisher of this book, and I will forward your letter.

Finally, if you wish to correspond with Sallie Ann Glassman or me, or if you are coming to New Orleans and would like to speak with either of us, please write to us in care of Inner Traditions.

GLOSSARY

Aché A term associated with Santería. The power of the Creator that flows through the universe; grace; blessing.

Bayou St. John The site in New Orleans of Voodoo rites conducted by Marie Laveau. Situated above the downtown area below Lake Pontchartrain.

Batá drums The three sacred drums used in some Santería ceremonies. They have two heads, one small and one large. The heads are surrounded by bells.

Bon Dieu Bon The Creator, the spirit that contains the will of all creation.

Calabash A gourd. The calabash is used to represent the head and destiny of a follower. The calabash in its stem and bowl combines the cup or chalice (female) and the wand (male) both of which are Western esoteric ritual implements.

Congo Square A square in New Orleans where enslaved Africans gathered and danced, at times under the direction of Marie Laveau.

Connaissance Esoteric knowledge; knowledge of or from the loa.

Cook To allow objects used in ritual to sit together for a length of time after the ritual. This mingles the forces called in the rite with the objects.

Dahomey A powerful West African kingdom, now Benin, which contributed greatly to the Voodoo liturgy.

Dr. John A Voodoo practitioner and drummer in New Orleans during the beginning of the nineteenth century.

Golden Dawn A Western esoteric order (c. 1888–1914), centered in England, which contributed greatly to the Tarot deck as it is known today.

Gros Bon Ange Large Good Angel. In Voodoo, that part of the soul that connects the voodooist with all of creation. Love as union. It is constantly in union with Bon Dieu Bon. The terms Gros and Ti Bon Ange are used interchangeably by different voodooists.

Guinée Africa in a real or idealized form. The Holy Land of the loa. The continent on which our species probably originated.

Head The part of the practitioner's anatomy where the loa or spirit indwells. A replica of a head used to house a sipirit.

Heat up To bring power into objects and participants through ritual, music, or other activities.

Hoodoo Probably derived from Voodoo. A set of healing and spell practices with a very practical orientation.

Hounfor A Voodoo temple.

Houngan Voodoo priest. A Fon word meaning "spirit chief." May be the head of a hounfor.

Hounsis Wives of the spirits; male or female initiates in Voodoo.

Legba A loa whose task it is to open the door to the other loa or spirits called in ritual. The other loa or spirits can not enter if Legba does not open the door. Legba carries the words of the voodooists between the visible and invisible worlds. He usually presents himself as an elderly, black male using a cane.

Loa African spirits that traveled to the New World with the enslaved Africans. Used interchangeably with "Mysteries" and "Spirits."

Macumba African-based spirituality as practiced in Brazil.

Madam L Alternate name for Marie Laveau.

Mambo Voodoo priestess; may be the head of a hounfor.

Mange sec Dry meal. These are sacrifices offered to the spirits without blood. All sacrifices offered in this book are mange sec.

Marie Laveau A New Orleans Voodoo priestess. She lived from 1794 to 1881 and is known for her occult skills and works of charity.

Marassa The Divine Twins of Voodoo. They are the embodiment of complementary duality. They are not actually loa and may perhaps best be described as a cognizant process. They are called and honored before the loa in Voodoo ritual.

Oriaté A Santería initiate; master of ceremonies.

Orisha Santería term for the African spirits that made the Middle Passage; a saint, in that the orisha have been syncretized with the Roman Catholic saints.

Sacrifice From the Latin *sacer* (sacred) and *facere* (to make). To sacrifice is to make sacred. *The New Orleans Voodoo Tarot* does not promote sacrifices involving any member of the animal kingdom. Leaves, branches, etc., used in sacrifice should be gathered in ways that respect the plant or tree from which they are taken. The earth should be thanked for all minerals gathered to be used as sacrifice. See also **mange sec.**

St. Louis Cemetery No. 1 The most widely accepted resting place of Marie Laveau and Dr. John, located close to Congo Square.

Root Doctor   A practitioner in the Voodoo or Hoodoo tradition who is knowledgeable in the use of roots to cure disease and cast spells.

Santería   A new-world religion based on the spiritual practices of the African Yoruba and strongly influenced by Spanish culture. The word itself refers to the worship of the saints, which are African spirits, syncretized with the Roman Catholic saints.

Thelema   A religion and philosophy that began with Aleister Crowley receiving *The Book of the Law* in 1904; a major school of Western esoteric thought.

Ti Bon Ange   Small Good Angel. That part of the voodooist's personality that gives rise to individual action; in effect, similar to the conscience. The will. The meanings of Ti and Gros Bon Ange are used interchangeably by various voodooists.

Vèvè   A ritual drawing used to call a loa or spirit. Each loa or spirit has its own vèvè. Traditionally they are drawn on the ground using cornmeal.

Voodoo   A term that has come to include the body of practices and beliefs of those who serve the loa.

Yaguó   An initiate in Santería.

Yoruba   An African people located in Nigera whose religion forms the basis of Santería.

BIBLIOGRAPHY

It is commonly believed that there is very little nonfiction dealing with the subject of Voodoo. This bibliography, while by no means exhaustive, provides the reader with a wide field of choice. No attempt has been made to identify the books in terms of their value, except for the exclusion of patently racist publications. The sample is biased enough in that the books are culled from both authors' libraries. An honest paragraph in an otherwise sensationally lurid book may do more to connect the reader with the loa than a generally excellent book that, while providing factual information, does not ignite the spark that bridges the gap between the reader and the loa. Also, a reading of some of the more questionable books can provide insight into the origin of popular misconceptions surrounding Voodoo. All of the books are in English. This excludes numerous publications in French. Sections listing books on Kabala, Tarot, and other related subjects are also provided.

The bibliography is extensive in order to provide those knowledgeable in Voodoo, Tarot, or Western mysticism with the means to gain further information on the other systems. So that the new reader in the Mysteries not be set completely adrift, *Divine Horsemen*, *Jambalaya*, and *The Qabalistic Tarot* make up an introductory trinity of books of lasting value.

HAITIAN VOODOO

Bach, Marcus. *Inside Voodoo*. Bobbs-Merrill, Reprint. Originally published in 1952 under the title *Strange Altars*. New York: Signet, 1968.

Bertiaux, Michael. *Voodoun Gnostic Workbook*. New York: Magickal Childe Inc., 1988.

Brown, Karen McCarthy. *Mama Lola: A Voudou Priestess in Brooklyn*. Berkeley and Los Angeles: University of California Press, 1991.

Courlander, Harold. *The Drum and the Hoe: Life and Lore of the Haitian People*. Berkeley and Los Angeles: University of California Press, 1960. Reprint. California Library Series, 1973.

———. *Haiti Singing*. New York: Cooper Square Publishers, 1973.

Davis, Wade. *The Serpent and the Rainbow*. New York: Warner Books, 1985.

———. *Passage of Darkness: The Ethnobiology of the Haitian Zombie*. Chapel Hill: University of North Carolina Press, 1988.

Deren, Maya. *Divine Horsemen: The Living Gods of Haiti*. London and New York: McPherson, 1953.

Dunham, Katherine. *Island Possessed*. Garden City, N.Y.: Doubleday, 1969.

———. *Dances of Haiti*. Los Angeles: Center for Afro-American Studies, University of California, 1983.

Herskovits, Melville J. *Life in a Haitian Valley*. New York: Alfred A. Knopf, 1938.

Hurston, Zora Neale. *Tell My Horse*. Berkeley: Turtle Island Foundation, 1983 (copyrighted by author, 1938).

Huxley, Francis. *The Invisibles, Voodoo Gods in Haiti*. New York: McGraw-Hill, 1966.

Laguerre, Michel S. *Voodoo Heritage*. Beverly Hills, Calif.: Sage Library of Social Research, 1980.

Marcelin, Philippe Thoby & Pierre. *The Beast of the Haitian Hills* (novel). New York: Time, Inc., 1946.

Métraux, Alferd. *Voodoo in Haiti*. New York: Schocken Books, 1972.

Reed, Ishmael. *Mumbo Jumbo* (novel). New York: Bantam Books, 1972.

Rigaud, Milo. *Secrets of Voodoo*. Translated from the French by Robert B. Cross. New York: Arco Publishing Company, 1969.

———. *Vè-vè*. New York: French and European Publications, Inc., 1974.

Seabrook, William B. *The Magic Island*. New York: Literary Guild, 1929.

Valdman, Albert. *Haitian Creole–English–French Dictionary*. Bloomington, Ind.: Indiana University Creole Institute, 1981.

Williams, Joseph J. *Voodoos and Obeahs: Phases of West India Witchcraft*. New York: Dial Press, 1932. Reprint. New York: AMS Press, 1970.

VOODOO—NEW ORLEANS/NEW WORLD

Gandolfo, Charles Massicot. *Voodoo in South Louisiana*. New Orleans, La.: The New Orleans Historic Voodoo Museum, rev. ed. 1987.

Gover, Robert. *Voodoo Contra*. York Beach, Me.: Samuel Weiser, 1985.

Haskins, Jim. *Voodoo and Hoodoo*. New York: Stein and Day, 1978.

Martinié, Louis. *Waters of Return: The Aeonic Flow of Voodoo.* Cincinnati: Black Moon Publishing, 1986.

——. "The Word in Praise of Legba," *Société Journal,* Vol. 2, No. 1, 1988.

Riva, Anna. *Voodoo Handbook of Cult Secrets.* Toluca Lake, Calif.: International Imports, rev. ed. 1974.

Saxon, Tallant, and Dryer. *Gumbo Ya-Ya: A Collection of Louisiana Folk Tales.* New York: Bonanza Books, 1945.

Tallant, Robert. *Voodoo in New Orleans.* Gretna, La.: Pelican Publishing Company, 1990 (copyrighted by author, 1946).

——. *The Voodoo Queen.* Gretna, La.: Pelican Publishing Company, 1983 (copyrighted by author, 1956).

Teish, Luisah. *Jambalaya: The Natural Woman's Book of Personal Charms and Practical Ritual.* San Francisco: Harper & Row, 1985.

SANTERÍA

Murphy, Joseph M. *Santería: An African Religion in America.* Boston: Beacon Press, 1988.

Rose, Donna. *Santería, The Cuban-African Magical System.* Miami: Mi-World Publishing Co., 1980.

Wippler, Migene Gonzalez. *Santería: African Magic in Latin America.* New York: Crown, 1973. Reprint. New York: Original Products, 1981.

——. *The Santería Experience.* Englewood Cliffs, N.J.: Prentice-Hall, 1982.

——. *Rituals and Spells of Santería.* New York: Original Publications, 1984.

MACUMBA, UMBANDA, QUIMBANDA, AND CANDOMBLE

Bramly, Serge. *Macumba*. New York: St. Martin's Press, 1977. Originally published as *Macumba, Forces Noires du Bresil* (Paris: Editions Seghers, 1975).

Langguth, A. J. *Macumba: White and Black Magick in Brazil.* New York: Harper & Row, 1975.

St. Claire, David. *Drum and Candle.* Garden City, N.Y.: Doubleday, 1971.

AFRICAN

Courlander, Harold. *Tales of the Yoruba Gods and Heroes.* New York: Crown Publishers, Inc., 1973.

Gleason, Judith. *Orisha: The Gods of Yorubaland.* New York: Atheneum, 1971.

———. *A Recitation of Ifa, Oracle of the Yoruba.* New York: Grosman Publishers, 1973.

———. *Oya: In Praise of the Goddess.* Boston: Shambhala, 1987.

Hunt, Carl M. *Oyotunji Village, The Yoruba Movement in America.* Washington, D.C.: University Press of America, 1979.

Pelton, Robert D. *The Trickster in West Africa: A Study of Mythic Irony and Sacred Delight.* Berkeley and Los Angeles: University of California Press, 1981.

Thompson, Robert Farris. *Flash of the Spirit.* New York: Random House, 1983.

Wippler, Migene Gonzalez. *Tales of the Orisha*. New York.: Original Publications, 1985.

KABALA

Fortune, Dion. *The Mystical Qabalah*. New York: Ibis Books, 1981.

Poncé, Charles. *Kabbalah*. Wheaton, Ill.: Quest Books, 1983.

Regardie, Israel. *A Garden of Pomegranates*. St. Paul, Minn: Llewellyn Publications, 1978.

———. *The Tree of Life*. York Beach, Me.: Samuel Weiser, 1980.

MAGICK AND MYSTICISM

Crowley, Aleister. *The Book of the Law* (also known as *Liber L*, *Liber AL*). London: Ordo Templi Orientis, 1938. Numerous reprints.

———. *777 and other Qabalistic Writings*. York Beach, Me.: Samuel Weiser, 1977. Numerous reprints.

———. *Magick in Theory and Practice*. Paris and London: privately printed, 1929–30.

Grant, Kenneth. *The Magical Revival*. London: Mullen Books, 1972. Reprint. London: Skoob Books, 1991.

Kemp, Daniel. *The Book of Night: Legends of Shadow and Silence*. New Orleans, La.: Iraya Press, 1990.

Linden, Mishlen. *Typhonian Teratomas: The Shadows of the Abyss*. Cincinnati: Black Moon Publishing, 1991.

Regardie, Israel. *The Complete Golden Dawn System of Magic*. Las Vegas, Nev.: Falcon Press, 1984.

Toups, Oneida M. *Magick High and Low.* Jefferson, La.: Hope Publications, 1975.

von Franz, M. L. *The Feminine in Fairy Tales.* Dallas, Tex.: Spring Publications, 1972.

Wendell, Leilah. *The Book of Azrael: An Intimate Encounter with the Angel of Death.* New Orleans, La.: Westgate Press, 1988.

————. *Our Name is Melancholy: The Complete Books of Azrael.* New Orleans, La.: Westgate Press, 1992.

TAROT

Case, Paul Foster. *The Tarot: A Key to the Ages.* Richmond, Va.: Macoy Publishing Co., 1947.

————. *The Book of Tokens: Tarot Meditations.* Los Angeles, Calif.: Builders of the Adytum, 1934. Reprint 1968.

Crowley, Aleister. *The Book of Thoth.* London: O. T. O.,1944. Reprint. York Beach, Me.: Samuel Weiser, 1990.

Falorio and Fowler. *The Shadow Tarot: Birthing the Dark Feminine Within.* (Book and Deck). Pittsburgh: Headless Press, 1989.

Kaplan, Stuart R. *Tarot Classic.* New York: Grosset & Dunbar, 1975.

Ashcroft-Nowicki, Dolores. *The Shining Paths.* Wellingborough, Northamptonshire, England: The Aquarian Press, 1983.

Waite, Arthur Edward. *The Pictorial Key to the Tarot.* Blauvelt, N.Y.: Rudolf Steiner Publications, 1971.

Wang, Robert. *The Qabalistic Tarot.* York Beach, Me.: Samuel Weiser, 1983.

JOURNALS & ANTHOLOGIES

Bahlasti Papers. New Orleans, La.: Kali Lodge, Ordo Templi Orientis, 1986 to present.

The Cincinnati Journal of Magick. Cincinnati: Black Moon Publishing, 1976 to present.

James, Darius. "A Black Man's Guide to Seducing White Women," *Bahlasti Papers*, newsletter of the Kali Lodge, O.T.O., in New Orleans, 1989. Soon to be published in *Love is Strange* anthology (New York: Norton Press, 1993).

Société Journal. Burbank, Calif.: Technicians of the Sacred, 1986 to present. Dedicated to the preservation and practice of Voodoun and other neo-African religious systems.

ARCHIVES

The Archives. Cincinnati, Oh.: Black Moon Publishing, 1983 to present. (Largest open occult archives. Issues lists of manuscripts and photocopies.)

The Archives. Burbank, Calif.: Technicians of the Sacred, 1988 to present. (Provides referrals only. Dedicated to the goal of the preservation of African and neo-African systems, religion, gnostic, and hermetic studies.)

(See the section on Contacts & Supplies for the addresses of these journals and archives.)

INDEX

(This index concentrates upon the introductory chapters and "The Cards in Practice" chapters. The Road, Spirit, and Temple cards can be located by using the detailed Table of Contents.)